THE INVISIBLE
INK SERIES

TEACHING FOR CREATIVITY

SUPER-CHARGED LEARNING
THROUGH THE
'INVISIBLE CURRICULUM'

ANDREW HAMMOND

First Published 2015

by John Catt Educational Ltd,
12 Deben Mill Business Centre,
Old Maltings Approach,
Melton, Woodbridge IP12 1BL

Tel: +44 (0) 1394 389850
Fax: +44 (0) 1394 386893
Email: enquiries@johncatt.com
Website: www.johncatt.com

ISBN: 978 1 909717 350

Set and designed by Theoria Design.

Contents

Foreword
by Geoff Barton

It's hard to argue against creativity. Most of us like the thought of creative people doing creative things. Perhaps even more we like uncreative people doing creative things – such as when unlikely staff members appear in a spoof music video. Students roar with laughter: they love the incongruity of their sour-faced physics teacher suddenly dancing Gangnam Style. We do too.

That's what I like so much about Andrew Hammond's approach to creativity. He doesn't do that classic knee-jerk of Creativity Defenders, setting creative stuff against academic stuff.

That's what we get too often in debate about education – the limiting and unhelpful myth that it's either creativity or rigour, that the two can't coexist.

Andrew Hammond shows that they can and do. He shows that opportunities for creative responses lurk everywhere – in any lesson and around the lessons. His view of creativity is rooted in the real world, and it's celebratory, not soppy; practical not ethereal.

Thus he explores opportunities for spontaneous creative activities. He explores how teachers can create contexts through planning. He illuminates the language we need in providing children with opportunities to make connections, respond to unexpected questions, to think more laterally.

It's all written with a lightness of touch and rich seam of anecdotes that makes it a charming and entertaining read. Don't be beguiled by the frothy surface, though: underneath there are serious points about how and what we teach.

The result is hugely informative, lively, engaging – and, yes, creative.

Geoff Barton
Secondary Headteacher and educational author
Suffolk, June 2015

1 Playing with buttons

The Proustian phenomenon tells us that our sense of smell has more power than any other sense to provoke distinct and emotional memories within us. In his novel, *À la recherche du temps perdu* ('In search of lost time') Marcel Proust describes a character vividly recalling memories from his childhood after smelling a tea-soaked biscuit. Memories, long-forgotten, can often come flooding back to us, when certain smells are encountered again.

A whiff of bacon and egg does it for me.

I am always whisked away to Weston-super-Mare, aged seven, going for a morning stroll with my Grandpa. At the end of his road, just near the sea front, was a nursing home for the elderly and every morning the most luscious smells of full English breakfasts would blast out of a vent in the kitchen wall. The seaside, for me, doesn't smell of seaweed, it smells of bacon.

Trips to Weston were always a sensory adventure. After serving in the war as a bomb disposal expert, my Grandpa turned his steady hands to chiropody and his surgery was inside the house. The unforgettable smell of phenol and salicylic acid would always greet us in the hallway after my Nana had opened the door with a beaming smile.

But the most memorable part of our weekends in Weston wasn't the chemicals or the bacon or the seaside. It was my Nana's old wooden button box – a large, rectangular open tray with a handle across the top of it. It was divided into several felt-lined compartments and each one housed the most extraordinary delights you could imagine. Shiny blue ones, pearly white ones, two holes, four holes, leather toggles, great big brass ones, tiny red spherical ones. Some so small you could imagine an elf sewing them on to a shirt, others so large they must have fallen from a giant's duffle coat. And then there were the military ones, my favourites, with emblems and crests and royal coats of arms. You could only imagine the places they'd seen, peering like eyes from the tunic of a sailor.

How I loved that button box. I'd spend hours rifling through it, listening to the clickety-clack of the little buttons rattling in the tray, running my fingers through them like sand on the beach beyond the nursing home. Watching the colours as I blended them all together into a multi-coloured, chunky soup. Laying them out in rows and creating patterns across the floor. Threading them on to string and making my Nana a necklace or my father a pretend wristwatch. Button men, button roads, button food and button jewellery. How could anyone resist their enticing appeal?

If you want a definition for what creativity is, and I guess any book of this title should begin with such a thing, then you need look no further than my Nana's button box. I have thought a great deal about why I was so transfixed by it – why hours would pass unnoticed while I was so absorbed. I've often mentioned that button box when delivering CPD training in schools and it's astonishing the number of teachers who smile and nod their head. It seems I wasn't the only one who liked playing with buttons. There is a common fascination in childhood for sorting and shaping and creating, isn't there.

I know now what I was doing during those trips to Weston. I was engaging in pure, unfettered creativity and I believe there were four distinct stages to it.

Firstly, I was using *perception*. I rifled, sifted, flicked and clicked. I swirled them around and studied all the colour combinations and varieties. I studied them with great care and interest. Their differences intrigued me – so many variables in one wooden box. I used my senses to get to know them all, see and feel them, hear them clickety-clack in my hand, become familiar with all the constituent parts of the creations that were to follow.

Secondly, I made *connections*. I loved nothing better than dropping them over the carpet and sorting them into different categories, coloured or plain, two holes or four, round ones, toggles, odd shaped ones, plastic or metal. There was something very pleasing and therapeutic about the practice of sorting them into groups. I remember, years later, I found myself working in a petrol station as a student. I used to tip the packets of cigarettes all over the kiosk floor just so that I could sort them out again (it broke the monotony of a night shift). Their different coloured designs pleased me and they stacked up so well together – making an ideal Jenga substitute during quiet shifts.

Back in Weston, there then followed a really exciting stage in my work with those buttons, the *synthesis* stage. I blended and connected and combined those buttons to create original designs and products, from sculptures and collages to roads, figures and jewellery. These were different every time and I was proud of them. They meant something to me and those buttons allowed me to give vent to my imagination in a physical way. The button box was a palette and I was the artist, synthesising the elements together with imagination and vision. It didn't occur to me that there was a wrong way or a right way to build a button man, or a button chain – so I wasn't afraid to 'have a go' and just see what I could make. It was the same with Lego, with which I am still besotted even now. Back then, of course, I would grab any pieces I could find from the giant tub of crusty blocks and knock up a vehicle, spaceship or hobbit's hovel from my imagination. Now, as an adult, I mindlessly follow Lego kit instructions and call it therapeutic.

After the synthesis stage came the final part, the *presentation*. This was the much anticipated 'ta-dah' moment, when I ran into the kitchen, grabbed my Nana, pulled her by the hand into the front room and said 'ta-dah! What do you think, Nana?' A rapturous response always ensued. Nana's arthritic hands were misshapen and twisted but I knew she had once loved playing with those buttons as much as I did and my elaborate designs never failed to bring a smile to her face.

The four stages of my button work were of equal importance, though I didn't realise it at the time. All I knew was there was a procedure to it, a kind of ritual that I always followed, enjoying each stage, and especially the last.

Perceiving, connecting, synthesising, presenting. You need all four stages for creativity to flourish in schools. And this book is about how to plan for each of them in teaching and learning.

The learning environment

In Book 1 of this series, *Teaching for Character*, I laid out the case for the invisible curriculum, upon which this series is based. I explained how historical assumptions about the purpose of school – to develop the academic intelligence of children and to demonstrate this via academic qualification, encouraged through rewards and sanctions – have created a learning environment that is non-conducive to the character traits and attitudes needed for success and well-being in life.

And the same is true for creativity.

The culture and climate of the formal classroom, predicated as it so often is on the fast and efficient delivery of a visible, academic curriculum with its examinable knowledge and skills, creates a place in which creativity is under-valued at best, and rejected at worst, or saved for an art lesson, period six on a Friday. Like other elements in the invisible curriculum (such as character, curiosity, motivation, cognition, communication and collaboration), creativity is of supreme importance to child development and preparation for adulthood, and yet it does not fall easily into a compartmentalised and examinable syllabus. Neither does it subscribe to the kinds of extrinsic rewards offered in schools – in fact, the intrinsic motivation to create may positively dwindle as soon as rewards are mentioned.

But it finds a way. If the visible curriculum is the carefully laid pavement, neat and square and measurable, creativity is the greenery emerging between the slabs. It is a natural force within all of us. It is a pressing need to do something original and it makes us human. It is pleasingly illusive and very difficult to trap. You can't teach creativity in the same way you can teach arithmetic or handwriting. And neither can you entice it with the promise of rewards. But you can work hard to stop putting things in its path. And you can recognise its supreme value in learning, working and living. You could even pull up a slab or two and place a garden there.

But like natural plants emerging through a man-made pavement, creativity can be seen by some as rebellious, non-conformist – a capricious trouble-maker. Creativity is so often associated with art, music or drama lessons, because these are seen as rightful places for it, taught by someone willing to let go of the reins a little and allow the children some autonomy. Arts subjects are big enough and quirky enough to find space for creative behaviour. Describing students, or even teachers, as having an 'artistic temperament' is rarely meant as a compliment, after all. The phrase is used to describe someone who is a mercurial free spirit, difficult to manage and difficult to discipline.

But creativity should not be seen as something so anarchical, devoid of rules or structure or discipline, like some unchecked, untrammelled expression of the soul with no regard for convention or skills. It should not be associated with hyper-sensitivity, unpredictability or a proclivity for mercurial outbursts. Rather, creativity requires tremendous self-discipline and structure. It requires a level head and a commitment to work hard. The artistic temperament we associate with 'the creator' is *passion* – when engagement is intense and drives all thought and action.

Creative expression also requires knowledge and skills in order to be articulated properly, and these most certainly can be taught. But creativity itself is not a linear discipline, learned gradually in incremental steps, all of which you have to master before you can consider yourself 'creative'. It is not reliant on a full mastery of skills before it can be expressed. You can be imaginative without having an extensive vocabulary or without being a master painter or sculptor. But you can get better at expressing your ideas and become more skillful at painting, writing, composing and so on. Creative skills can be taught.

But at creativity's core, lies imagination and you can't teach that. Fortunately you don't need to, of course – children are factory-fitted with it from birth.

This series is based on the fundamental belief that any attempts to create formal schemes of work and accompanying assessment criteria for teaching the 'invisible curriculum' will be counter-productive. Rather, we should look more closely at the optimum *learning environment* needed for the invisible elements of human development – what I term 'invisible ink' throughout this series – to flow freely. This invisible ink is, essentially, what distinguishes us as humans: our capacities, aptitudes and attitudes; our imagination; the energy that flows through us – our lifeblood. And it requires the right learning environment in which to flow.

I have identified six key features of the learning environment that will help us to facilitate, monitor and report on invisible ink effectively in schools, and this includes children's creativity. These features I define as:

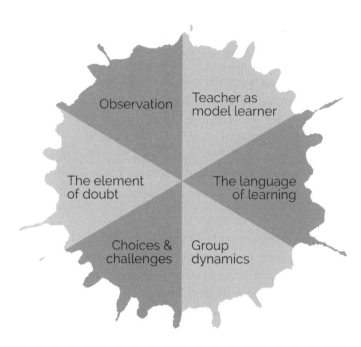

Figure 1: Six key features of the learning environment

Creativity, just like character, curiosity or motivation, is not best developed through a formal curriculum and assessment programme. The skills required to express one's creativity – perceiving, connecting, synthesising and presenting – may be taught from a curriculum, and their proficiency assessed, and they already are, of course. The work of great artists, authors and musicians can be studied and mimicked. But imagination, creative thinking, inventiveness, having the courage to be original, these qualities don't sit easily inside a scheme of work or assessment programme. They require the right *growing conditions*. These six features of the learning environment will help us to ensure we don't teach pupils out of their creative zones – because they will need their creativity when they are older, as much as they will need their arithmetic and their handwriting ability.

Or perhaps they'll need it even more.

2 Perspectives: Teaching for creativity

> Creativity is too flexible and too capricious a phenomenon to be easily defined. (Kneller, 1965: 1).

Like the children themselves, creativity is an unpredictable, whimsical concept to set down. When a person is 'being creative' he or she may encounter a very personal moment of revelation when connections become clear, ideas are synthesised and something novel is created. Such epiphanic moments are subjective, ephemeral and, by their nature, unique, so categorising or describing them is difficult. Freud said creativity originates in a 'conflict within the unconscious mind'. So not only is an internal moment of creative inspiration difficult for observers to understand and report on, such an epiphany may even be difficult for the creator himself to express in words. Bernard Golden (2007) also writes about the unconscious element of the creative process:

> At its best, true creativity is characterised by collaboration between your conscious and unconscious mind. You can consciously work at being creative, but you are also dependent on your unconscious mind, that part of your psyche over which you have no direct control, to provide inspiration. (Golden, 2007: 23)

What does 'being creative' actually mean? There are as many different interpretations for this phrase as there are colours in an artist's paint box. We can agree that one's imagination needs to be involved in some way for an activity

13

to be considered 'creative'. And there needs to be an element of novelty, or originality. But what else? Does it require something visible to appear on a page? Something visual on a stage or audible in a concert hall? Does there need to be an end product involved every time?

Sir Ken Robinson's definition for creativity has become well-established these days – 'the process of having original ideas that have value'. It is useful that he refers to a process here, rather than a product. In the much-quoted, seminal report, *All our Futures*, by the National Advisory Committee on Creative and Cultural Education (NACCCE) in 2000, chaired by Sir Ken, creativity is defined thus:

...imaginative activity fashioned so as to produce outcomes that are original and of value. (NACCCE, 2000: 4)

Originality and value are key here. Of course, neither may seem in abundance for the teacher who is marking children's acrostic poems on the theme of Autumn for the twentieth time. The imagery within the lines produced by the children may have been seen by the teacher a thousand times before, but the originality and value is there for the creator too. If the child has produced something new to them and valued by them, then it must be creative, mustn't it?

But does imaginative activity, or 'being creative', necessarily mean generating a product, ready to exhibit or perform? In my own explanation of the four stages of creativity offered in the previous chapter – *perceiving, connecting, synthesising* and *presenting* – the third stage clearly involves the construction of *something*. But does this something need to be a physical piece of work that can be seen and judged? Or can it be an idea, an imaginative thought or a novel solution to a problem?

Writing a poem, painting a picture, learning a piece of music or rehearsing for a play: clearly these pursuits are creative as they are creating something original and of value, though not always – I'm thinking here of certain rehearsals I have watched in certain schools, where the children have been grilled, drilled and filled up with what to do, what to say and how to say it, and I'm left wondering how creative the experience actually was. But the end product itself is not as important as the process, as the story of the sergeant major drama teacher shows. Schools so often miss this. They produce a school production of *Oliver* or *Joseph and his Amazing Technicolor Dreamcoat* that will enthrall parent audiences and remind them why they chose this school to send their children to, without realising that the military-style drilling and rehearsing may have driven out any sense of being or feeling creative. This is not, perhaps, the best example of being creative at school. But it does produce a very creative spectacle, filled with colour and music and lights and lots of excellent acting and very clear diction, audible from the back of the room.

But what of the other opportunities to be creative that exist across the school curriculum? We cannot rely on performance and visual arts to be the only oases of creativity in a desert of academic rigour. There are, of course, plenty of ways to be creative in other subjects too, and in the spaces between those subjects. As Mathilda Marie Jourbert (2001) reminds us:

> The arts are often termed 'the creative arts'. This is a serious misnomer, since the arts can sometimes be taught or practised in very uncreative ways, and mathematics, history or literacy can be taught in highly creative ways.' (in Craft [ed], 2001: 23)

But there is a potential dichotomy here in that schools are built around a curriculum, which in turn is built around knowledge to be delivered and received, skills to be modelled and mimicked and established truths to be believed. As Anna Craft (2005) writes:

> There are potential tensions between the existence of a curriculum with a great deal of propositional knowledge, and the encouragement of pupil – and teacher – creativity.

There is an agenda in schools, perhaps linked to those historical assumptions again, in which the curriculum and its accompanying assessment programmes are everything. The teachers are the purveyors of content and the students are the recipients. There is much to be taught and learned, and which will ultimately be examined.

But, as every good teacher knows, it needn't be a one-way street. Effective teaching and engaged learning involve more than mastery of the three Rs of receiving, retaining and regurgitating; it is a proactive, two-way dialogue: a shared discovery, in which the children's own contributions are as valuable as the teacher's – precisely because they not only give us insight into what they do or do not remember of the knowledge we've taught them, they also give us an inkling of their ability and willingness to respond creatively to that knowledge: to take a position, to make connections and to construct their own interpretations.

To this extent, this book is not only concerned with teaching for creativity, it is also concerned with how *creative* teaching and learning can lead to better performance and better grades – precisely because the learners are more engaged when they are 'being creative'. When learning moves from a passive receiving of knowledge to an active grappling, scrutinising and interpreting it, that is when deeper understanding is gained. When the children are given opportunities to use their sensory perception, to make connections, to construct something for themselves and to present it to others, then I believe this leads to active, meaningful learning.

Being actively engaged in the learning process – as creators themselves – means that knowledge is retained and understood more deeply by the students, because it has been applied; it has been used to create something original and of value, from a re-enactment in history, to a story in English or a 3D model in maths. It means more to the learner.

When, a few years ago, I devised the *Independent Curriculum*, published by Galore Park, (later called the *IC Programmes for Learning*), I was keen to develop a model for creative teaching and active learning that did precisely this, to take the canon of knowledge one might expect from a good education and map it against a series of cross-curricular learning skills that meant children were not only receiving knowledge, they were discovering it, applying it creatively and then presenting it.

I was inspired at the time by a quote from the prodigious creator himself, Leonardo da Vinci: 'I've been impressed by the urgency of doing. Knowing is not enough, we must apply. Being willing is not enough, we must do.'

This has huge significance for us as teachers, the purveyors of knowledge. In Book 1, *Teaching for Character*, I wrote that da Vinci proudly described himself as an *Omo Sans lettere* – an unlettered man, which he saw as being uncluttered by the mimicry and indoctrination of a formal education. I can connect with his references here to *applying* and *doing*. These are wholly active occupations.

So in the *Independent Curriculum* (IC) I wanted to give children the opportunity to discover new things, apply them to create something new and then to communicate what they have learned with, and to, others.

So I created a framework in which each gobbet of knowledge or concept was put through a series of actions or 'learning skills'. These were:

Discovering   Applying   Communicating

I couldn't find a subject within the curriculum that did not, in some way or another, encompass these learning skills. The purpose of the IC was to develop children's knowledge and understanding of the taught curriculum *at the same time* as developing their curiosity, creativity and independent thinking – precisely because the learning activities provided in the IC made for a very *active* learning experience.

My thesis was always that it's not just the knowledge you teach, it's the way you teach it, and the learning skills practised along the way are as important as the knowledge itself – or perhaps even more important.

This, in some way, helped to address the dichotomy of which Craft writes above, because it was developing generic learning skills that are very valuable to the creative process, rather than the didactic model of teaching a lot of knowledge but without facilitating much applying or doing. I don't think children become creative just by listening and watching and mimicking, no matter how creative the teacher at the front of the class may be. They need to do it for themselves – the learning experience needs to be an active, multi-sensory one. As Novak (1998) writes:

> The creative performance of everyone can be enhanced by improving the capacity and desire of people to learn meaningfully. It is retarded or inhibited by inordinate emphasis on learning by rote. Because the latter has been so common in most school learning, it is not surprising that the biographies of geniuses often refer pejoratively to their experiences in schools. (Novak, 1998: 74).

Of course the children need to be formally taught the skills of composition, design and expression, but so too do they need to be given the chance to imagine.

You can rote-teach a monkey how to hold a paint brush or use a fountain pen, but without an imagination it's hard to create a picture or story that is original and of value. (No offence to monkeys, there may be some deeply imaginative monkeys out there who, unluckily, have not yet been taught how to hold a paint brush).

There must be opportunities throughout our formal teaching to invite the children to respond creatively to what we are teaching them, and to put the skills we are giving them into action. 'You've learned how to ride a bike, now go for a ride yourself' (being careful to stay close to home, of course, and take your mobile phone with you and don't talk to strangers and tell me what time you'll be back *etc*). One must keep this book current and the days of 'Mum, I'm off out on my bike, back for tea' may seem dated, I realise, but the metaphor still works.

The playfulness of creativity

The aforementioned report from NACCCE tells us:

> There needs to be a balance in all good teaching between formal instruction of content and skills, and giving young people the freedom to inquire, question, experiment, and express their own thoughts and ideas. (NACCCE, 2000).

Giving children the freedom to express their own thoughts and ideas sounds like something few teachers would disagree with – of course they need to have the chance to express themselves – but in practice things can be very different. The very word 'teaching' conjures up images of children sitting behind desks and a teacher at the front of the classroom talking at them whilst clutching a wooden ruler and pacing, just as the word 'teacher' evokes thoughts of a tall person standing over a sedentary shorter one.

It's hard to move teaching on from these stereotypical views that belong in Mr Gradgrind's school room, because it is the experience of many parents and grandparents, even still. Every good teacher knows there are times to be a sage on the stage and other times when it's better to be a guide at the side. Creativity is one of the latter moments, when we are facilitating and sharing in the children's discoveries and creative endeavours. One can demonstrate the skills in didactic fashion, but one needs to stand back and let the children use those skills to explore.

There is a playfulness about creativity, a fidgetiness that may seem disobliging in the formal classroom, and challenging to manage. In his superb book, *How to Catch Lightning in a Bottle* (2006), George Gamez defines creativity as 'a return to the playful child within us'.

Is there space and time for such playfulness at school? Perhaps there is a second dichotomy here – school restricts the times when children can 'play' to playtimes and yet we know that creativity requires one to be in a playful state of mind. Isn't it interesting that we often use the word 'playtime' to mean the space in between lessons, which in turn are the periods reserved for *working* and definitely not playing.

If we look at children in a playful state, at 'playtimes', they are engaging in all the valuable activities and showing all the valuable attributes we might expect for creativity to flow: courage, freedom to express themselves, possibility thinking, collaboration, imagination, role play, exploration, improvisation, daringness.

If we consider the attitudes and behaviours children present when in a work state in the classroom, they may look markedly different: fearful rather than courageous, compliant, obedient, sedentary, requiring direction and guidance, unsure and awaiting instruction.

But we are in danger of dealing in extremes here! Not all classrooms look like this. There are plenty of attributes that are common to both a work and play state, provided the work is engaging enough and some *active* learning is going on. Creativity not only requires a playfulness and a freedom to explore or experiment, it also requires determination, grit, focus, structure and discipline, and all of these are required for study too. Perhaps it is when we feel that creativity is about playfulness and rebellion only that we do not welcome it into our formal lessons and relegate it to the playground instead.

But playtime proves that many children, when left to their own devices, are creative by nature. Perhaps all children in way or another? The key is this element of being left to their own devices. This need not mean being physically abandoned! It means the passing of just a little bit of ownership to the child.

When the child feels that there is little or no chance of owning any of the lesson content, be it writing, drawing, making or plain thinking, then I doubt there will be much real creativity going on. When the teacher sets the work, establishes the expectations, the format, the time and the success criteria, when she marks the work and gives the feedback on how they did, compared with what she was expecting and had envisaged they would do, then, in what way is this the children's work? In what way do they have ownership of the words or images they are producing?

But there is another aspect of lesson time, beyond the question of ownership, that may stifle creativity even more. In fact, it can kill it. It is the fear of *getting it wrong*. The maxim, if at first you don't succeed, try, try again, is so apposite to our cause here. Creativity demands the courage to experiment and see what you end up with. As educational author, Robert Fisher, tells us:

> Creativity, like evolution and education, is founded on experimentation, variations that sometimes succeed, sometimes fail. (Fisher, 2004: 8)

But the aforementioned historical assumptions about the purpose of school may have created a learning environment in which it is good to succeed, and bad to fail. This may mean that at the very point when a child is struck by some creative impulse, she may pause before she articulates it to see if it is 'right', to see if it will meet with the teacher's approval and match to up expectations, or the approval of her peers. Will it fit with the lesson objective or be as good as the exemplar piece modelled at the beginning of the lesson? What will it say about the student? Will it say she is too keen, or not keen enough? Will it make her look daft or, even worse, very clever? (I will discuss such worries further in Chapter 5: Group dynamics).

Being creative, by definition then, may result in failure or success. There are risks involved in creating whilst in a crowd – a danger to it, and the culture of the formal classroom only magnifies that danger.

But this wasn't the case when the child was younger, of course. Before attending formal school, she would have engaged in imaginative play and improvisation and untrammelled exploration effortlessly and without caution, whether anyone else was with her or not. Playing and 'making stuff up' is what little children do, it's their job, after all. I don't know many children who need to be taught how to play. (Granted, they may need to be taught how to play fairly and nicely, and sensibly, but they don't need to be taught how to pretend or how to turn a stick into a sword).

It reminds me of a treasured moment shared with my eldest son in those heady days before we were required to strap a tie up to his neck and call him a pupil. It was a long summer and to occupy him we played in the garden with anything we could find.

One afternoon I found myself outside with him once again. He saw a couple of sticks lying under a tree. He picked them up and threw one of them at me. Keeping the other and pointing it in my direction, he lunged towards me and said, 'Ah ha! Captain Hook. Do you want to have a battle?'

I willingly obliged, of course.

Henry started formal school in that autumn. I will always remember the following summer when I ran into the garden once again and grabbed a pair of sticks. I gave one to him and then chased him around the garden, shouting 'So, Peter Pan. We meet again!'

Henry stopped in his tracks and said, 'Daddy! That's a stick not a sword. It rhymes with 'brick' and did you know it begins with the letter pattern 'st', like *st*one and *st*op.'

'Gosh, son,' I said, 'How interesting.' And at that moment something died inside me. I knew that Henry had entered the formal world of meaning-making. Nothing would ever be the same again. And it wasn't. He had left the land of metaphor and make-believe and travelled to a literal place where spelling patterns and meanings were deemed to be more important than potential, figurative meaning, symbolism and imaginative play. What something means, how it is made and what it is for – these would be the things that would occupy his thoughts from now on. The naming of parts. Pretending something is something else, using it to construct imagined realms and to project fictional roles on to someone else, like his Dad, would now be filed under the heading 'play', which Henry had already worked out in his mind was somehow not as important as 'work'. The fact that he was so keen to tell me that he had learned something at school – how 'stick' is spelled and what it is for (or not for) – suggested to me that he valued his new knowledge, perhaps more than he valued his ability to consider, playfully, the 'stickness of the stick' and use it as a springboard to another world. That was just playing – what little kids did. He was bigger now.

Granted, this is an odd example, because one can just imagine a teacher at playtime telling Henry in no uncertain terms that 'a stick is not a sword!' but it makes the point and it is all absolutely true. The day Henry went literal and learned that stick begins with *st-*.

Beyond the literal world

If we are to encourage children towards creativity, we must re-engage their sense of the possible, the different, the off-the-wall. We must not give them the impression that anything and everything is certain and beyond other interpretations. I return to this subject in more detail in Chapter 7: The Element of Doubt.

The stick story reminds me how the potentiality of words, and objects, is such an important concept when teaching for creativity. I was teaching at the time and so when I returned to school after that summer, I devised a fun lesson starter which was my humble attempt to counter all this literal meaning-making, which I felt sure was closing down possibility thinking rather than encouraging it.

I sat the children in a circle. I presented a pencil to them – just an ordinary pencil. Without saying anything by way of an introduction (always a good way of getting their curiosity tingling) I held the pencil carefully in my hands, closed my eyes and said, 'In my mind, I can see, the object in my hand could be.... a meerkat's walking stick.'

There was much laughter and not a little incredulity as they thought, not for the first time, 'Sir's lost it again.'

I said, 'Right. Your turn. Go on. Who's next?'

A couple of brave children thrust their hands into the air (I have to say, the ones who always jabbed their hands into the air no matter what the question, and whether they knew the answer or not). But give them their due, they delivered. They understood, without my prompting, what the game was.

The first child came and took the pencil from me, sat down and said, 'In my mind, I can see, the object in my hand could be... a giant's toothpick.'

'Brilliant!' I said.

Others took turns and soon we were able to pass the pencil around the circle, one by one, taking it in turns to shut our eyes and thoughts to the literal meaning of 'pencil', to feel the 'pencilness of the pencil' and conceive the possibilities of what else it could represent. From an English language point of view, this is pure metaphor making.

I remember on another occasion I brought in a basketball. We passed it around the circle and we shared lots of interesting possibilities: a giant marble, a space ship, a speck of dust because we were all microscopic. And then came the turn of a particularly shy boy who rarely spoke up in public arenas like this.

He held the ball and screwed his eyes shut. I said gently, 'Don't forget, you're welcome to pass if you want to. Anyone can say pass and we can come back to them another time.' But he kept hold of that ball and wouldn't move. The circle went quiet and I felt a sinking in my stomach as I worried that this would result in him feeling embarrassed and even less likely to speak up ever again.

And then he spoke up.

'In my mind…. what was it again?'

'I can see,' I prompted.

'Okay. In my mind, I can see… what was next?

I told him.

'In my mind, I can see, the object in my hand could be… erm…erm…wait a minute…erm…'

The room fell silent. We looked at each other nervously, so desperate for him to dislodge something in his mind, anything, and cough it up.

Silence. Just red cheeks. A couple of sniggers from somewhere in the circle. A frown from me. Still silence. And then,

'… I'm a giant and this is a planet,' he burst out, turning the ball quickly on his finger tips, 'And look, it's a spinning planet.'

I don't know if he would ever have had the chance to demonstrate the size of his imagination like that had we not played the game. It became *his* game. Whenever we played it, no matter what the prop, we all looked forward to hearing what he would say next.

Four stages to the creative process

I liked the making metaphors game especially because it dealt with our perceptions. In fact it played with them. We could all perceive that the pencil was just a plain old pencil, but using our mind's eye we could consider how the 'pencilness of the pencil' gave it the potential to symbolise something else. We were building connections, transferring meanings – making metaphors.

Perception and connection. If you remember, these were the first two stages in the creative process I offered in Chapter 1. I concluded that it involves four stages and these are:

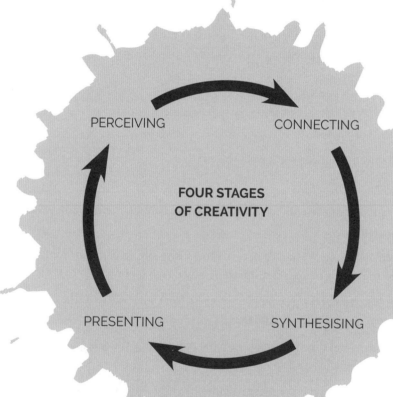

PERCEIVING

CONNECTING

FOUR STAGES OF CREATIVITY

PRESENTING

SYNTHESISING

Figure 2: The four stages in the creative process

From a teaching point of view, this is indeed a virtuous circle because each stage leads on to the next, and the final stage of 'presenting' is what the children then perceive from others, then base connections upon, then use to construct their own ideas and so on. So as teachers we are presenting much of the curriculum to them, after we have used our own perceptions, made our own connections and constructed what we are going to present to them, be it a talk, a worksheet, a piece of writing or something else. They in turn perceive it, build connections and so on. Round it goes.

But this four-stage process requires a little magic – a spark of inspiration to set it going. We hope that in the classroom that spark comes from our presentation to the children – be it a talk, movie clip, sound, or some other stimulus which the children then perceive and draw connections from. Without that epiphanic moment the creator may lack the most important driver of all to create – their self-motivation. The self-motivated creator will be prolific. I am reminded here of a delicious quote from the American writer and novelist, Pearl S. Buck:

> The truly creative mind in any field is no more than this: A human creature born abnormally, inhumanly sensitive.
>
> To him...
> a touch is a blow,
> a sound is a noise,
> a misfortune is a tragedy,
> a joy is an ecstasy, a friend is a lover,
> a lover is a god,
> and failure is death.
>
> Add to this cruelly delicate organism the overpowering necessity to create, create, create – so that without the creating of music or poetry or books or buildings or something of meaning, his very breath is cut off from him. He must create, must pour out creation. By some strange, unknown, inward urgency he is not really alive unless he is creating. (quoted in Inglesias, 2001: 4)

I believe the drive to create, create, create which Buck refers to here comes from a flash of inspiration, a moment that ignites the creative process – setting it alight. These moments must be generated as often as possible in school. But they are rarely created through reasoned discussion; the senses need to be involved. In my experience, when the learning is multi-sensory, the children may very well unearth that nugget of an idea which drives them on to create. They feel it more keenly. There is an intrinsic need to solve a problem experienced, articulate a feeling felt or share a response to what has happened to them. They may have seen something, heard something, witnessed a spectacle or experienced a feeling so strong that to express it becomes an absolute necessity, otherwise they might burst.

Finding inspiration

When my son Henry was about seven years old we took him, his little sister, Nell, and his even littler brother, Edward, to Portsmouth to visit HMS Victory. For the sake of accuracy, we took our fourth child, Katherine, too, but she couldn't see the Victory from inside her mother.

It was a bright, sunny day and as we entered the Royal Docks and walked around to the quayside, the great bumblebee-coloured ship, in all its majesty, came into view, its proud masts thrusting into the azure sky and its decks punctuated by little black cannon barrels. It was jaw-droppingly pleasing to the eye.

I turned and whispered, 'And you can go on it.'

Henry's face was a picture, as was everyone's. 'What?' he said, incredulously, 'You mean we can *actually* climb aboard?'

His use of such a nautical term was charming and I gave him a smug grin and a wise nod, as if to imply, 'Yes, but only because your Daddy has managed to pull a few strings and speak kindly to the Captain, or Admiral, or someone in a pointy hat anyway.'

We rounded the corner and promptly saw a queue of brightly clothed students, with even brighter knapsacks, waiting impatiently, snaking right up the staircase and into the ship itself. Clearly Daddy had not fixed a private audience, but my children's excitement was unabated.

A marvellous day was had. The sights, the sounds, the smells, all combined to create a sensory adventure that none of us would forget. The cannons, the hammocks, the giant ropes curled up like sleeping serpents, the Admiral's dining room, the men's lowly quarters, and the prison cells below them: it was extraordinary.

But what happened later that day was even more intriguing.

We returned home and Henry rushed into my study (to which I had retreated as soon as we were back, as ever) and promptly asked me for some paper – 'lots of it, please!'

'Of course, what do you need it for?'

'Oh, I'm just writing some books, you know.'

'Oh, of course,' I said. 'Well, take as much as you need.'

He grabbed a stash and tore off like a dog with a bone. I was determined not to shoot his fox and seek to find out any more about the project before he'd even started. Why do we so often do that? We see children are clearly planning something exciting and so we ask them what it is. Let them build the suspense, I say. Don't ask them to reveal it until they're ready. It diminishes their motivation to do so.

A couple of hours later I couldn't resist having a peek, however, and so I went up to his room. The carpet was a sea of paper sheets, some ripped up and others crinkled like crests of waves. He was sat at his little desk writing furiously.

'What're you writing, son?'

He didn't look up, tongue hanging out, salivating with gleeful determination.

'It's a book. About Nelson.'

'Oh, brilliant.'

'And when it's done, Daddy, I'm going to write another one about the Victory ship. And then another about Portsmouth Royal Docks.'

'Tremendous, son.'

I tiptoed out, trying not to disturb his creative flow (much more on that later). As I reached the landing, he shouted out, 'Oh, and Daddy? Do you have a dark blue jacket I could borrow?'

I returned to his room. 'Of course.' (The temptation to ask what he needed it for was immense, but I resisted).

'And a cushion, please?'

'Erm, yes.'

'I'll need to take the stuffing out of it though,' he said. 'Is that alright?'

'Oh… of course. Whatever you need. Just remember to stuff it all back in there when you've finished. And don't tell you mother I said you could have it.'

'And some empty toilet rolls. I'll need lots of them.'

'No problems. Wash your hands afterwards, won't you,' I said, swallowing a chuckle and returning downstairs.

About an hour later and Henry was standing proudly in the kitchen before the rest of the family, wearing my jacket (draped to the floor), an empty cushion on his head fashioned into an Admiral's tricorn hat and clutching a long, cardboard telescope up to one eye.

On the work top next to him was a completed book entitled *All About Nelson*.

The next three days were the most prolific of Henry's life so far – and still to date. He created not two more but four more mini-books, all carefully illustrated and telling the intriguing tale of Horatio Nelson, and of his ship, and of the Royal Docks, and of the sausage, chips and beans we'd enjoyed in the restaurant.

The sensory adventure had heralded something special in Henry and it led to a frenzy of inspired, creative activity.

It is difficult to boil down such an inspired and prolific period into a word or phrase, but I shall call it 'creactivity': the surge of creative endeavour that follows a moment of enlightenment, which has been inspired by an immersive, sensory adventure. There should be more creactivity in schools, rising from sensory experiences like our trip to Portsmouth. It's an ugly word, but it fits our purpose well enough. Creactivity.

Henry was not churning out these illustrated books because he was instructed to or because he was tempted by the promise of extrinsic rewards if they were any good. Neither was he following some exemplar that I had modelled for him. Having been given the stimulus that prompted his epiphanic moment – the trip to Victory – he was pretty much left to his own devices. He wrote these books because he *had* to and if he had not done so he would have undoubtedly popped.

Making time for 'creactivity' in school

The writer, W. Somerset Maugham, famously said of authors, 'We do not write because we want to; we write because we have to.' I can understand this, and so can Admiral Henry.

The intrinsic motivation to create, create, create was almost tangible in my son at the time and it was a pleasure to witness. His creactivity produced a plethora of books and pictures and role-playing.

I have witnessed plenty of such creactivity at school, as have most teachers. It often follows a 'real-life' experience – a school field trip, a walk through the woods, a visit from a travelling theatre company, a science experiment or a sporting event. Anything that sees the children up and exercising their bodies and their senses.

I recall one day some years ago when I was reading David Almond's wonderful *Skellig* with a Year 6 class. We were reading the chapter in which Michael visits the dilapidated garage at the bottom of his garden for the first time (the place where he was to discover the old man with wings):

> Something little and black scuttled across the floor. The door creaked and cracked for a moment before it was still. Dust poured through the torch beam. Something scratched and scratched in a corner. I tiptoed further in and felt spider webs breaking on my brow. (Almond, 1998: 6)

The children enjoyed reading the chapter together. I then asked them to leave their books behind and follow me. We left the classroom, went winding our way through corridors, down a flight of steps and then, eventually, to the cellars of the main school building. It was a place as close to Michael's garage as I could find. There was plenty of dusty clutter and spiders and dark shadowy corners framed in cobwebs. (No, I don't recall completing a risk assessment sheet for our little trip down there, in case anyone asks, and I'm sorry for that).

I asked the children not to touch anything at all but just to look, and smell, and feel the atmosphere down there. It was musty and dark and the dim light bulb on the wall left unexplored dark places that seduced the imagination.

We spent a good few minutes down there, talking in whispers and soaking it all up.

When we returned to the classroom I asked the children to create mind-maps and record on to them words and phrases that would do the cellar justice. I did the usual trick of drawing a hand on the whiteboard. They knew that this signified our five senses – an *aid-memoire* to remind them not to restrict their imagery to what they had seen only, but to consider how their other senses had been tingled too. Of course, the hand I draw always has six digits – to include our 'sixth sense'. (We have Aristotle to thank for suggesting we have five senses. In truth we have many more. The latest suggestion is twenty-one, though I'm sure we have an infinite number). As I have already suggested, our sense of smell may be our most evocative and so I would emphasise to the children the need to write about what they smelled down in that cellar.

The power of smell is most easily illustrated using a doughnut.

If ever I smell doughnuts – the deep-fried, sugary kind one buys from the back of a van at a fairground – then I am instantly whisked away to Scarborough in the 1980s, enjoying an Easter holiday with my family. I cannot say the same images are so vividly conjured up if I *see* a doughnut, or if I *touch* one, or if some trickster walks up to me unexpectedly and whispers, 'Doughnut.' This is enough proof for me – smell trumps the lot.

And yet I wonder how much attention this sense receives in the classroom? How much sensory learning actually goes on at school? Learning should be an aesthetic experience after all, but I wonder if formal schooling turns it into an anesthetic one? Children should have their senses sharpened in school, not dulled – because as sure as anything, many of them have their senses numbed at home at the mercy of the video games they play.

Back in the classroom, after our brave venture to the dusty depths of the cellar, I encouraged the children to create a repository for their responses to the cellar trip using a mind map or word bank. I could tell the children were eager to record what they'd experienced on paper. Creactivity beckoned.

These maps, and the creative prose that followed, was filled with sharp and evocative imagery. And what's more they didn't want to stop writing when the bell signaled breaktime, which I always see as a good sign. Many of them remained in the classroom for a while longer, desperate to set down on paper the experience they had enjoyed down in that cellar. Something had touched their senses and plenty of creactivity followed as a result.

Seizing the moment

I don't claim to have done anything particularly new here; it would be absurd to suggest so. Most teachers will have treated their class to similar sensory adventures from time to time, I've no doubt. The quality of the creative writing, or painting or musical compositions or role-playing that follows is always impressive, isn't it. And the intrinsic motivation to give vent to their emotional responses to such adventures is equally astonishing, provided you can seize the moment and get them writing or painting or composing whilst recollections of their experience are still fresh in their minds. The children who had visited the cellar were fully engaged, driven on to express themselves creatively, not because of the promise of rewards, but because they had to get it out and on to the page, or else they'd burst.

But I wonder how many times when we return from a school trip we encapsulate the experience in a chronological recount of 'our day out'. We use it as an opportunity to teach time connectives or the use of paragraphs or the past tense or something like that. We pin learning objectives to such a task that often relate to language techniques prescribed in the curriculum, which risk overshadowing the untrammelled creative outpouring that is creactivity. To some extent, perhaps we preset the format for their written responses to those sensory adventures – word count, structure, inclusion of certain key phrases and so on. The freedom so necessary to creativity is slowly driven out by the conditions and criteria we place on their work when they get back to school.

I think for creativity to survive through school, one needs to immerse the children in sensory adventures of this kind and then allow them time immediately after to pour out their emotional responses to those adventures – in the form of free writing or artwork or drama or music. When we deliver these experiences we are, in effect, creating a little space in which the children are 'left to their own devices'. We are creating scope. The trip to see HMS Victory, or even the little adventure down to the old cellar at school, broadened the children's perceptions but it also broadened the parameters for how they could respond. Let's face it, there is a myriad different ways we can react to a dusty, spidery, cobweb-filled cellar. But there are not so many different ways we can react to a spelling test or a maths question. That's just the point; in fact, there is only one correct way. Spelling and maths are supremely important, before anyone suggests I am advocating we drop them from the curriculum, but so is the sensory adventure, and especially for creativity.

Sharpening children's senses is an important aim for school, and so too is putting those sensory experiences, and the creative inspiration that immediately follows them, into a form so they can be shared with others. In her book *Letting the Buggers Be Creative*, Sue Cowley puts it succinctly:

> Inspiration acts as a stimulus to the creative parts of our minds. This part of the process is probably best described by using a metaphor. If undertaking the creative journey is driving a car, then the inspiration stage is the act of turning the key to start up the engine. (Cowley, 2005: 24)

I think it is too much to ask children to express themselves creatively on demand and without the necessary spark plugs. One can jump start them with a worksheet comprising some creative lines to be continued, or exhibiting the creative work of someone else for them to mimic, but this is never going to be as useful as enabling them to start up their creative motors themselves. And that means inspiration, which often needs a sensory adventure.

Fortunately children are rarely short on creative inspiration. I don't know where it comes from and I don't know why it comes. I assume it is part of what makes us human. But every child has the capacity to be creative and be inspired, provided we don't place obstacles in the path of such creative flow. But unfortunately the aforementioned literal naming of parts – the mechanical teaching of language and numbers and meanings can so often close children's minds to possibilities and potential meanings and original interpretations.

I wanted to take that stick and wave it threateningly in front of the person who taught my son that 'stick' begins with 'st-' and rhymes with 'brick' and that's that. But this is a preposterous reaction on my part, because his teacher was doing just what we expect them to do – teaching my son how to read and write.

Seeing things differently

When my daughter, Nell, was small enough to perch on my shoulders, I took her for a walk down by the canal near our home. I'm sure such practices are frowned upon these days on health and safety grounds – walking so close to water with a small child perched on your shoulders, and without completing a risk-assessment sheet? – whatever was I thinking? It seemed fair enough at the time.

We'd been walking for a while when suddenly Nell began shouting excitedly and jabbing her mini Kicker boots into my collar bone.

'Look, Daddy!' she said. 'Dinosaur bones, I can see dinosaur bones!'

I said, 'What? I'm sure there aren't any dinosaur bones, darling. Whatever do you mean?'

She just giggled and said, 'Can't you see them?'

I set her down (at a safe distance from the canal, you understand) and started scratching about on the ground like a chicken. My shoes scuffed the earth, in search of what I assumed would be the bones of a bird or rabbit, dispatched and then discarded by a ravenous fox.

But I just couldn't see any bones. All the while Nell kept silent apart from the odd mischievous giggle.

'Okay,' I said, 'I give up. Where are these bones? I can't see any. Are you sure?'

Eventually she put me out of my misery and said, knowingly, 'Not down there, silly. Up there. Look!' She pointed a tiny finger up to the sky. And there, sure enough, was a giant cloud that had been stretched across the sky by the breeze and then chopped up like a diced carrot by cross winds. And if that wasn't the cast of the diplodocus skeleton that greets you in the foyer of the Natural History Museum, then my name is Dippy. It was an almost exact replica from where we were standing. Nell was right.

But it had never occurred to me, a literal adult schooled in the naming of parts and meanings, that such bones might be in the sky rather than on terra firma. After all, how can you find dinosaur bones in the sky! It doesn't make sense does it. So I didn't bother looking for them there. But as W. B. Yeats once said, 'The world is full of magical things, just waiting patiently for our senses to grow sharper.'

This true story illustrates how important it is for us to retain our own sense of the possible, the off-the-wall, the metaphors that lie all around us. There has been much written about how children's metaphoric competence dips in the primary years, after such a promising start in the early years, when they shift effortlessly between real and imagined realms.

Creativity in school requires an open mind, free from the usual cynicism and obsession for the literal, rational way of thinking. How many of us, as pupils ourselves, were prevented from gazing out of windows and day-dreaming? And yet legend has it that Albert Einstein was day-dreaming one summer's evening, whilst sitting on a hill. He was gazing at the sun's rays as they struck the Earth and imagining what it might be like to sit on a sunbeam and ride it past the planet. It is said that this day-dream gave rise to his theory of relativity.

One can just imagine young Albert drifting off in the middle of a geography lesson, and then being told to 'Stop dreaming and get on with your work!'

However you view creativity, whatever it means to you, it is an essential part of learning and growing and it needs to be encouraged rather than inhibited in the formal classroom. As I have said, I don't believe any teacher is motivated by the prospect of teaching children out of creativity, but the historical assumptions as to the purpose of school may be placing obstacles in its path by creating an learning environment that is non-conducive to the untrammelled flow of original thoughts and ideas so necessary to the creative process. This book is about how we can realign that learning environment using the six key features of the learning environment.

Removing the obstacles

Before we look in more detail at these features, permit me one further example of creativity in flow. A number of years ago I caught an interview on Radio 4. It was the actor Ewan McGregor and he was talking about his role in the extraordinary film from the ultra-creative, Tim Burton, *Moulin Rouge*. McGregor sings in the film and although he had sung before in his life, this was a big song and a big deal. It was Elton John's *Your Song* and he recalled how nervous he had felt about performing it in front of the cameras with his co-star, Nicole Kidman.

He trained for the part with a singing teacher and his account of the training he'd been given was intriguing. To paraphrase, he said his teacher removed the obstacles that prevented him from singing, so that he could simply 'sing'. Listening to him perform the song, one can see that's exactly what he is doing – just singing and it seems effortless somehow.

(How fitting it is that the song itself took Bernie Taupin just ten minutes to write whilst having scrambled eggs one morning at Elton John's mother's house. Presumably he too had removed the obstacles to writing and just simply 'wrote it').

I met a golfing pro once, some years ago. I asked him for some help with my swing. I'll never forget his words. He placed the ball at my feet, pointed to the flag in the distance and said, 'Right, Andrew, there's the flag and there's the ball. Now, hit the ball towards the flag. There's nothing stopping you.'

I like this philosophy very much and I think it may resonate for many teachers. We must remove the perceived obstacles that often lie in the path of children's creative flow, so there is nothing stopping them from creating.

Such obstacles might include: low self-confidence, poor self-belief, lack of optimism, apathy, low self-esteem and worry that what they create won't be any good anyway. It is rare for such obstacles to include a lack of talent, in truth.

But of all the obstacles in the path of a child's creativity, surely the most destructive is the aforementioned *fear* – fear of getting it wrong, fear of disappointing others and of not living up to expectations, fear of looking daft, fear of screwing it up and ending up with nothing, fear of being misinterpreted, fear of scoring a low mark, and so on. And yet these fears are entirely learned emotions, they are something children pick up from working in a formal learning environment and from doing so in a crowd. I don't believe such fears were there from birth, factory-fitted. I've heard it said that all of us are born with just two fears as a matter of fact, and they are the same in everyone: a fear of falling and, curiously, a fear of snakes. No one was born with a fear of looking stupid in front of their friends, or scoring the lowest mark from the teacher, or making a mistake or simply being wrong.

Which leads me to conclude that everyone is born to be creative. It's a much quoted cliché these days, but I'm sure Picasso was right: 'Every child is born an artist, the problem is how to remain an artist as we grow up.'

No-one is better placed than a teacher to ensure that children's innate creativity survives their school years, because it is the teacher who is architect of the learning environment; and it is the learning environment that will have the greatest impact on a child's motivation to risk everything and be original or play it safe and conform.

In the chapters that follow, then, I shall address how the creative process of perceiving, connecting, synthesising and presenting, can be best facilitated using each feature of the learning environment, which you will remember includes: teacher as model learner, group dynamics, the language of learning, choices and challenges, the element of doubt and observation. In each case, obstacles will be removed and children's creativity will be encouraged to flow.

Creativity needn't mean chaos

When I speak to teachers and school leaders about making space for creativity in their teaching and learning, the concern that comes up more frequently than any other is that creativity necessarily leads to a lack of structure and yet schools are, by design, structured places, so it can pose difficulties for lesson management and behaviour control. The effects of the creative process may worry some teachers, understandably; there is a heightened tension when creative inspiration comes. As the aforementioned Bernard Golden describes, in his interesting book, *Unlock your Creative Genius*:

> During moments of creative flow you react on a physical level. You feel energised, and may even experience the subtle changes in breathing that often accompany such tension. At times you may notice a leg shake, a finger tapping, or your tongue periodically darting against your teeth. These physical responses are symptoms of a nervous energy, a tension that is predominantly one of excited exploration against a backdrop of low-level, threatening anxiety. (Golden, 2007: 23)

Such 'excited exploration' is what we want in schools but it comes at a price, in terms of behaviour and control in the classroom. Do we really want children to be so fully engaged in the creative process that they are in a heightened state of excitement and even anxiety? Do we really want to risk excitable behaviour in our classrooms? Do we want to abandon all structure and boundaries just so that children can 'be creative'? And how on earth do we track progress in this regard?

We are at risk of the usual over-steer here that always comes when talking about teaching and learning, and the effects on behaviour when one style is preferred over another. Yes, some art lessons may seem noisier and a little more frenetic to a passing onlooker than, say, a maths lesson in which the children are working silently through a sheet of sums. But I've seen many maths lessons where the children are up and about, designing some 3D shapes or measuring anything that stands still long enough to drape a tape measure over it.

The point is that when children are allowed to be creative they feel a greater involvement in the process. This may manifest itself in a livelier disposition but this in no way need threaten the authority of the teacher in the room, or challenge the school's code of conduct or behaviour policy. I believe that when children are locked into some creative process they are, actually, far less likely to challenge the boundaries of acceptable behaviour than when they are sedentary, feeling disengaged and bored, listening to some monologue from the front. There is a fundamental difference between silliness born from feelings of boredom and lively, spirited behaviour which is driven by a creative outburst. Children are more likely to remain on task and focused if they feel ownership of what they are doing and see the point of it. The pressing need to give form to one's creative ideas can be a regulator in itself, keeping one focused and on-task. It brings its own sense of purpose. When a 'eureka moment' comes and a creative idea forms, there is very little that will distract children from the task of expressing that idea. They are not presenting difficult behaviour, they are creating!

Structure, order, remaining on-task, these things need not be enemies of the creative process. Rather they are necessary ingredients, especially when they are self-imposed by the creator himself. Our role as teachers is to create the conditions and stimulations that give rise to those epiphanic moments of creative inspiration. And when we do, we may find that the children will bring their own sense of purpose and concentration and hunger to finish the job. As teachers, our role is to facilitate that creative flow by removing the obstacles that may be prevent the child from following through on their ideas – the aforementioned fear, apathy, lack of self-confidence, distraction from peers and so on.

Creativity raises engagement

Does creativity have a place in the formal learning environment? Yes it most certainly does, but rather than allowing it to rise up between the paving slabs of an established curriculum, it needs to be embraced as a tool for raising engagement, increasing motivation and enhancing concentration, precisely because of its power to engross the children. Creativity enhances understanding, it doesn't obstruct it.

There may have been a time, perhaps, when creative activity was dangled like a bag of Haribo in front of the children when wanting to get them to knuckle down and complete some particularly knotty arithmetic or essay. 'If you behave yourself and work hard on your literacy and numeracy this morning, we'll have an art lesson this afternoon, and 'get creative'.

But I don't believe any teachers think like this today, any more than the children's parents do. The value of creativity has been much emphasised in recent years, not only in terms of engaging children's interest and developing imagination, but with reference to the very high value placed on creative thinking and innovation in the workplace. The creative industries inject such huge revenues into our economy and there is no doubt that creative skills are highly prized by employers in a wide range of industries and professions. The UK is a global leader in the creative industries.

School leaders and teachers all know the importance of preserving and developing children's ability to solve problems, think creatively, perceive new solutions, make new connections and construct original designs. And every good teacher recognises the power of creativity to raise engagement and interest in learning. Nurturing creativity and maintaining academic rigour are no longer seen as mutually exclusive goals in education today. You raise academic standards when you unlock children's creativity in the classroom.

But I do believe the structure and practices of formal schooling may give an impression that academic rigour matters more than creativity. Look at the timetable: an hour's literacy and an hour's numeracy every day, usually in the morning, with subjects considered to be more creative relegated to one lesson per week in the afternoon. As a former Director of Studies, I remember dolloping out that most treasured commodity, time, to the academic subjects first, ring-fencing their obligatory four or five hours of lesson time per week before then considering how to distribute the last few vestiges of time among arts-based subjects.

This will always be the case. But a recurring theme through this book will be how every subject can embrace the disciplines, attributes and attitudes of the creative process because of the benefits they bring to academic progress too. Every subject can benefit from the high engagement, energy and enthusiasm that is generated in pupils when creative activity is incorporated into lessons, whether they are reserved for maths, languages or humanities.

Unless or until creativity is seen as a pursuit that requires a disciplined, structured approach, rather than a practice that is synonymous with a thrilling sense of chaos and liberty, then it will always be relegated to half-hour periods of drama, dance or art.

This book will enable you to bring creativity into the formal learning environment in a structured and sensible way so that it not only develops children's imagination and artistic skills, it raises academic standards and impacts positively on all learning precisely because of the disciplines, attributes and attitudes which are modelled in the creative process.

Creativity need not mean disorder and chaos. By creating the right learning environment, one can promote, monitor and report on *structured creativity* right across the curriculum.

3 Teacher as model learner.

Like all aspects of children's invisible ink (the aptitudes and attitudes that impact on their learning and growth) creativity is encouraged in school as much through osmosis as it is through direct instruction. It's infectious. A teacher filled with the energy and enthusiasm to be creative will instill the same behaviour in her pupils. A teacher who values creativity encourages her pupils to value it too. You can teach children the skills and structures that will help them to give vent to their creative ambitions and impulses, but the most effective way to give rise to those ambitions in the first place is to be energetic and ambitious yourself. Time and time again children learn most effectively not from the things you say or the instructions you give them, but from the *person you are* and the behaviour you model. Creativity is no exception to this rule.

This chapter will take the four stages of creativity – *perceiving, connecting, synthesising* and *presenting* – and consider what opportunities there are for the teacher to model these activities for her pupils in the classroom and around the school environment. Throughout the chapter, as with the whole book, I will be pressing home the need to be self-motivated at all times, because it is your own motivation to create that will rub off on the children more than anything else. As the DfE's Teachers' Standards explain, we must 'demonstrate consistently the positive attitudes, values and behaviour which are expected of pupils.' As teachers we are model learners and we are best placed to personify the creative behaviours we seek in the children. This is the most effective way to encourage creativity to flow through our schools.

1. Perceiving

Leonardo da Vinci, who will play a leading role in this series, largely due to my growing obsession with him, said 'All our knowledge has its origins in our perceptions.'

This seems a rather obvious statement in one sense, although it could be taken as one that advocates empirical learning over a rationalist approach. I shall resist the temptation to follow the well-trodden path of pitching a rational, reasoned approach against an experiential one, or an academic, curriculum-based education against a child-centred, play-based learning experience, since clearly *both* are valuable and necessary teaching styles. For as long as the western world is focused on learning through formal instruction and logico-deductive reason (Robinson, 2001) and for as long as we prize conscious, explicit, deliberate, logical thinking (Claxton, 2008) above anything else, then such a debate is 'academic' anyway (note, the term 'academic' is often used derogatively to describe something that is not rooted in reality or of no practical use).

This book will not present an 'either/or' scenario: *either* academic rigour *or* creative expression; cognitive *or* non-cognitive, empirical learning over a rationalist approach – because I have never seen these as mutually exclusive goals. Whether or not schools were originally built for the sole purpose of disseminating propositional knowledge in order to boost the 'academic intelligence' of their pupils, most of us know now that it is in the synthesising of academic instruction with sensory, creative experiences that the most gains can be made and the clearest understanding is achieved and felt.

The effective learner is *perceptive*, and this applies as much to the teacher as to the student. When the teacher enjoys learning through their perceptions, then this in turn may 'switch on' the students to their senses too.

So, as model learner, the teacher needs to be tuned into their powers of perception – to be consciously aware of sensory experiences as they happen; to avoid living in their head only, and using their body to transport their brain from one lesson to the next. This is how many of us adults function and it sets a poor example to young learners.

Sensory learning means paying attention to how our senses are influencing our brain wavelengths, our mood and our general disposition and willingness to learn.

There are various 'creative habits' we can model for the children that will aid their creativity and encourage them to value their powers of perception, as we do:

Play music

Music is a very clear example of this. Do you play music quietly in class while the children are working, reading or creating? You will often find background music in an art room or a CDT workshop (or resistant materials laboratory, if that's what they're called these days).

Music of the Baroque period has been proven to have the greatest benefits to the learning brain; such music pulses at between 50 to 80 beats per minute and this has been found to stabilise mental, physical and emotional rhythms, which greatly supports concentration. The music of Vivaldi or Handel, for example, can stimulate creativity, since it creates a relaxed mood and removes the stressors which so often impede creativity. Many of us think more clearly and are less prone to the little insecurities and anxieties that foil innovative thought when we listen to music.

Try it, and you might just find it's true.

I have tried many different types of music in class (mostly instrumental as I find lyrics can distract) and have found that Baroque music never fails to bring a calmer, more positive and certainly more productive atmosphere. And, whilst playing it, I am showing the children that I value the effects that music can have on the way we think, create and learn.

Use colour

I am a great advocate of using colour as much as possible in the learning classroom. I remember, as a Director of Studies, I was charged with the task of writing the timetable for the school. I recall the first task I did was to change the way the timetable was presented to the teachers and children on the walls of classrooms and corridors. I insisted that it was shown in colour (up until then it had been in black ink only). I gave every subject its own colour and every member of staff had their own colour too – their initials appearing in a little coloured box. The mixture of coloured letters on a coloured background provided enough different combinations to give everyone their own identity.

I received several comments from both staff and pupils that the timetable was easier to read and easier to follow. Of course, such lovely colour did not, unfortunately, alleviate the tension when room clashes were discovered, as they always were in the first week of term.

I decided that if a multi-coloured timetable works well, why not use more colour in other areas of the classroom, so from then I presented lists and notices and records and all manner of information in a multi-coloured way. It was astonishing how many more children seemed to take notice and actually read the displays.

Colour is one of the first building blocks we use to discern different shapes and objects around us, so presenting information in colourful ways is tapping into children's innate capacities to learn and process information. And besides, much of the information we need to communicate in schools via notices and displays can be monotonous, can't it. Colour makes it a little more appealing – provided we don't over do it and bombard the children with a cacophony of colour!

Colours have more impact on us than perhaps we may realise. Different colours have been found to stimulate different emotions within us: *blue* is a cooling, soothing colour, promoting concentration and lowering blood pressure; *green* is also seen as a calming colour, alleviating stress; *red* can stimulate a faster heart beat and evoke stronger emotions within us; yellow can prompt the release of serotonin in the brain, which creates a feeling of happiness – this in turn can increase the brain's processing speed and promote rapid thinking and planning. A combination of red and yellow together has been found to stimulate our appetite. Several fast-food companies spring to mind.

Notice the weather

The weather has such impact on learning, doesn't it, and being perceptive means noticing and talking about the changing seasons and climates. Watching children in a playground on a windy day is always interesting – one can clearly see how the weather impacts on our mood and on the atmosphere in the classroom.

Notice subtle changes in the weather on the way to school and make a mental note to discuss this in class. Patches of early morning mist, drizzly rain, cloudless skies, unseasonal frost, blustery wind – all of these elements have an enormous impact on learning and on the creative person's spirit, so discuss them in class.

We cannot deny that we are affected by the weather in this country, rather it aids our creativity, evoking emotional responses within us that need articulating in words or shapes or music. A dank and dreary morning in mid January needs talking about. Surely one cannot start a lesson without acknowledging that it's a cold, miserable day, but then offering a rallying cry to beat the weather by creating a warm, positive atmosphere inside! Being perceptive means not only noticing weather, but noticing the effect which the weather has on the children's mood and attitude to learning on a given day. Children are, by virtue of being human, highly sensitive creatures and we cannot round them up, put them in a classroom and talk at them without first making reference to the climate they experienced on the way there. When the classroom becomes a vacuum, divorced from the environment around it, we risk switching children's senses off, not on.

You might wish to give the children the task of coming up with a word to describe the weather during their journey to school each morning, and you can join in too. Then, when taking registration, you can invite the children to share their word rather than trot out the usual, mechanical response, 'Good morning Miss'. Their new responses may give you an insight into their mood for the day too!

Catch the spontaneous

Things happen in schools that one doesn't always expect. It can seem, sometimes, that circumstances conspire to distract the children from their course. A bird will fly into the window, a wasp will sneak in and wreak havoc, the wind will blow a branch down, someone will sneeze impossibly loudly, hailstones may rattle or a child will laugh so uncontrollably they break wind.

These are the things that are memorable, whether you like it or not. They resonate more loudly in the children's consciousness than much of the scheduled teaching and learning, no matter how stimulating we have planned it to be.

Being a model perceptive learner, means noticing these moments and drawing inspiration from them (with the obvious exception of the last example).

Expecting the unexpected and capitalising on it when it comes is part of being creative. Promoting creativity means embracing spontaneous moments of disorder and chaos, rather than planning and scheduling them out of the teaching and learning experience. Control is important, and behaviour management is an issue, I understand, but as I have stated earlier, the children are far more likely to disrupt and fidget when the learning is predictable and dull. To ignore a spontaneous moment is to encourage it to go underground and give the children something to chatter and giggle and wonder about in the subtext of the lesson, rather than as a headline. Either way it is still all they will remember.

The show must go on, of course, but equally, as a model learner we can show the children that creative responses can rise from the most unlikely and often unexpected moments. It depends whether our senses are on receive or switched off at the time. Being alert to learning, and to the unexpected moments that delight our senses, is to remind the children what it means to be human, and I can't help feeling that this is a good thing. I have said earlier that education needs to be an aesthetic experience and yet so often it is an anesthetic one. Perhaps much of this is due to the great emphasis placed on applied logic and computational capacity. The great obsession we have in schools on training children in the dark arts of verbal and non-verbal reasoning, arithmetic and the mechanics of grammar spelling, causes us to place extreme value on *concentration*.

I have a problem with this. I am not against concentration, of course not. Creativity itself requires enormous concentration – often called 'flow-state' these days. There should be more flow-state in lessons.

There are times in everyone's life and work when concentration is important. A heart surgeon, a pilot or a concert pianist spring to mind. And any job requires one to engage in extended periods of concentration from time to time. The children must be able to focus on the job in hand without being distracted and without fidgeting. No question.

But concentration on academic work, such as arithmetic or verbal reasoning, means shutting off that which makes us human: our sensory perception, our instinctive reactions to the environment around us, our ability to sense dangers or threats, our skill in seeing opportunities and chances, our ability to feel empathy, concern, love, compassion, anger, resentment, hostility. The list is endless. And yet none of these skills and perceptions are being developed in a lesson on applied logic or code cracking. Rather they are unwelcome.

That is not to say that verbal or non-verbal reasoning requires no creativity; of course it does, in the problem-solving and pattern-seeking and code-cracking required. Such tasks require tremendous perception, connection and synthesis.

But they do not require the heightened state of sensory perception that I am talking about in this chapter. Rather, they require children to shut off much of their innate perception in order to concentrate on a very small, very particular problem.

Modelling sensory perception in a broader, wider way means embracing any spontaneous changes in the environment around us *at the same time* as focusing on the learning going on. We can do both. We are not machines and we would do well not to encourage children to think that they are – walking and talking receptacles for a computational brain.

There is a range of different things we can concentrate on! It is worth practising in class. Give the pupils time to concentrate on their hearing ability, for example. Or take them outside and concentrate on smells or sights or atmospheres. Concentration in schools often seems to be associated with pupils' reasoning ability – or their arithmetic skills. Or their listening ability. 'Concentrate, you're not listening!' I remember those words from my own school days. Invariably I was concentrating, but not on what the teacher was droning on about. It was less exciting than the bird dancing at the window or the horizontal rain drops or shifting clouds, or the crumbling rubber in my hand or the wart on my finger or the doodle in my diary. Don't tell me I don't know how to concentrate!

Concentration is often used as a way of keeping control and I suspect no teacher is immune to the fears of losing control of the children's behaviour or attention, and seeing a lesson disrupted by unwelcome distractions. There must be an agenda and a sense of purpose! I favour the phrase 'curated curiosity', suggesting that we steer the children's perception and curiosity and allow them moments of exploration and creative impulse without allowing them to be too diverted from the learning agenda! Balance is key.

Promote many senses

As I mentioned in the previous chapter, we have Aristotle to thank for the suggestion that we possess five senses only. Current estimates are that we have at least twenty-one, which seems wonderfully specific, doesn't it.

There is *chronoception* – our sense of time. A favourite game in schools is to challenge the children to estimate when a minute is up. It is surprising how accurate some guesses are, and how wildly out others are. We also have a sense sometimes that time is dragging or, conversely, that time has flown by.

There is *nociception* – our sense of pain. Or *thermoception* – our sense of temperature. And *proprioception* – knowing where your own body parts are, instinctively (a sense often challenged by a police officer seeking to know if a driver is under the influence of alcohol). It is this sense that enables us to scratch an itch on our leg without ever needing to see our leg. Then there is our *equilibrioception* – our sense of balance. And there are many more. It is worth investigating this with your students. They may be surprised when you suggest that they have more than five senses.

Perhaps most interesting of all is what we often call our 'sixth sense': when we have a sense of foreboding that something odd is about to happen, and it does; or when we get a sense that a relative is about to telephone us, and they do; or when we enter a room and can sense that its occupants have just had an argument, even though we had not seen or heard them fighting. These senses cannot all be the same 'sixth sense', surely. In truth, I believe we have incalculable extra senses and as a model learner it is worth reminding the children of these extraordinary, extra-sensory perceptions.

As an English teacher and author of fiction, I take great joy in writing to appeal to readers' extra senses and I encourage young writers to do the same. When describing a story setting, one need not feel limited to its sights, sounds and smells, one can describe the atmosphere and its effect on the characters within it.

Modelling active perception for the children means staying alert to our environment and the physical phenomena around us, and being in tune with how we respond to these stimulations. There are obvious opportunities when this can be modelled more effectively than others – on school field trips and walks, for example – but there is still plenty to sharpen our senses in the classroom if we stay alert.

2. Connecting

All the definitions I have read on creativity suggest that it involves creating something *original*, but there is much consensus that the ingredients one uses to construct those new creations – be they physical components or abstract ideas – are very rarely new in themselves. I believe creativity is a process of rearranging information that comes to us into something fresh. And it's fundamentally about building connections.

In an interview with *Wired* magazine in 1996, Steve Jobs said:

> Creativity is just connecting things. When you ask creative people how they did something, they feel a little guilty because they didn't really do it, they just saw something. It seemed obvious to them after a while. That's because they were able to connect experiences they've had and synthesise new things. (Jobs, 1996: 102)

The sense of guilt which Jobs talks about is very interesting. There is a suggestion here that the creator has not actually created anything original, because the ingredients he used were not original in themselves; the creator just saw a new way of combining or connecting those ingredients. Jobs says 'they didn't really do it, they just saw something'. From this we can interpret he means they saw a new way of combining information or ideas so that in their synthesis something new was created.

Leo Ann Mean, in his book, *On Creativity: Awakening the Creative Mind*, agrees with this view:

> A creative idea is a combination of previously unrelated ideas as in Idea 1 + Idea 2 = Idea 3. Creativity is the process of relating, connecting and sometimes adding ideas to what is not previously thought of. (Mean, 2006: 5)

So seeing connections which perhaps others have not seen, is the essence of creativity and children need opportunities to do this. If we look back to my Nana's button box, we see that although the creations I was constructing were different every time, the ingredients – the buttons – never really changed. It was always the same box of buttons. But something caused me to see things differently each time I visited – I rearranged them into new combinations and patterns. I put different buttons together and produced different results. What I did not do, as far as I can remember, is learn how to make buttons and start making new ones. But even if I had, the materials I would have used to make those new buttons would themselves have been made by someone or from something else. So again,

I would be synthesising existing materials to fashion something original with them. It is still about making new connections.

The same is true of songwriting, for example. The notes, the chords, the words have all been heard before in one form or another. But it is the connections we make, the blend, the unique synthesis that makes a song original. And often the simplest blends are the most effective. I try to write songs on my guitar from time to time and I am always envious when I hear a new song on the radio, very simply crafted but offering a blend of notes or words that no one has quite offered before. The singer-songwriter makes it sound so easy. That is the genius isn't it.

You may be a songwriter yourself, or a painter or a writer, or a devilishly good button model maker. You may be one of the nation's army of crafters, fashioning cards and bags for you and your family. Or you may not, as yet, have found the medium which excites your creativity. Or perhaps you've just not had time, yet.

Whether or not you have the time and inclination to 'create, create, create' as Pearl Buck says, you will be making connections every day. The value, from the children's point of view, comes from doing so consciously so that you highlight how the connections have been made. This chapter includes several such ways of seeing and making connections which you can model for the children.

You are the model learner, modelling the process of making connections so that the children can pick it up themselves. Using Steve Jobs' take on creativity, you have an advantage over the pupils – you have much more experience on which to draw and on which to make those connections. Experience is such a useful ingredient for creativity, precisely because you have seen and felt and heard connections in the past, and can synthesise them to make something new. An artist who has been painting for many years may not necessarily be a better painter than the artist who is fresh out of art college, but he will have more experience to draw on, more connections buzzing around his head, he may see more possibilities. Just as a crime novelist may find it easier to churn out her fortieth novel than someone writing their second book, because she is so well versed in blending and connecting and synthesising. (Notice I say second novel, as the first is straightforward, it's the sequel that can have you stumped). Of course, there is always the danger that the prolific painter or novelist or songwriter will become entrenched in a certain way of blending and connecting that their work can become formulaic and predictable!

Creativity is very much a case of trial and error, and you have trialed more combinations and probably seen more errors than the children have. You don't need to be very experienced in order to create something new, but it helps.

You have experience but, as an adult, it may well be that you lack something that the pupils have in abundance, ironically: the *courage* to look at things differently. An open mind. If you recall the example of my daughter seeing dinosaur bones in the sky, here she was able to see something entirely fresh and make original connections which I would never have thought of, because I was more cynical, more literal. I did not think for a moment there was a possibility of dinosaur bones being in the sky so I didn't look there. It didn't make sense to look up. And if there's one thing we adults like, it's for things to make sense.

It seems a pity that just as we reach a stage where we have lots of experience upon which to draw and make connections, we lose the open mind and playfulness of childhood – and are less open to the possibilities of seeing things differently. My daughter was able to make connections which had never occurred to me. And that is what a model learner needs to do. The very best creative thinkers share a thought which seems very obvious to us all, but none of us had thought it until that person had shared it. Don't you love it when that happens? When you hear a statement or a musical phrase which seems so resonant, so instantly recognisable, but none of us were thinking it or humming it until we heard it. That is the true test of a creative master, to make the connections which perhaps many of us could have made but we simply hadn't. That's just the point.

The combination of adult teacher and student should, then, yield a plethora of creative ideas and products, precisely because you have a synthesis of years of experience and they have an open mind to see things differently, to break convention (or be totally unaware of it in the first place).

The teacher as model learner demonstrates making connections and reminds the children that it's something they do all the time, in the course of daily life. They may just need reminding of this.

Making metaphors

The children may be surprised to learn that they are making connections all the time in the language they use every day. Look at the world of metaphors. We all make connections and associations without perhaps even knowing it.

Take *ontological* metaphors, for example. These are a type of metaphor in which simple, physical objects are used to represent more complex emotions or abstract thoughts. Take anger. Once you know that confusion is most often represented as ball of string, then you begin to realise the phrases you hear and use all the time:

I've lost the thread; can we unpick this; I'm in knots here.

Similarly, anger is most often represented as liquid in a test tube:

I am at boiling point; you need to simmer down; I've got steam coming out of my ears; just cool down... etc.

Or 'love is a burning thing', as Johnny Cash once sang.

As model learner, point out these connections to the children and encourage them to make new ones. They could make new metaphors – new connections – to represent other abstract feelings, such as jealousy, nervousness or fear.

Another type of metaphor which is part of our daily language but the children may not have made the connection yet is the *orientational* metaphor. This is where an abstract feeling is oriented on a line to aid our understanding of it. For example, happiness is always up and sadness is always down:

I'm over the moon; I could jump for joy; I feel really high; I'm buoyed up.

I'm down in the dumps; I feel low today; I'm on a downer; I feel down.

Encourage the children to forge new connections to represent other feelings and create brand new phrases, for example loneliness could be outside and having company could be inside, or fear could be down and confidence could be up; or loyalty is here and disloyalty is over there.

Brand new metaphors created as a result of these new connections might include:

Loneliness: I'm locked outside; I'm far away; I feel removed; I feel distant;

Company: I'm safe inside, I'm in the building, I've arrived; I'm in the warmth

Fear: I'm so far under; I'm below the line; I'm crouching; I'm diving deeper.

Confidence: I'm flying; I'm rising higher; I'm towering over you; I'm up there.

These are not metaphors that have been made before, they are new ones but, of course, they are using language that already exists. But the associations – the connections – are new.

Making metaphors is a very specific example of what it means to make connections and think creatively. There are other examples which you can employ on a daily basis, just in the course of classroom life. One such example is in the learning objectives you plan for a lesson.

Communicating learning objectives

'Learning objectives' are common place these days and it seems sensible practice to focus the children's minds on a specific gobbet of knowledge to be learned, concept to be grasped or skill to be practised at the beginning of a lesson. One can assess the degree to which they have managed this at the end of a lesson and this helps them to feel a sense of accomplishment, which in turns promotes confident learning next time.

But there is an opportunity to encourage connection-making in the way this learning objective is communicated to the children. Why not do it cryptically? Or as a quiz, or a word game or treasure hunt? Giving children the opportunity to see and make connections is hugely beneficial to their creativity and it awakens their problem-solving ability and creative thinking early on in the lesson. It increases engagement and builds curiosity.

There are plenty of other ways to be a model learner for making connections. One might wish to participate in word association games, such as word tennis, for example – where two players hit an imaginary ball across a net. The 'ball' is a word associated with an agreed word family or category. When a player repeats a word gone before or hesitates with an 'erm' then their opponent wins the point. This is making connections.

There are numerous other word games one might play with the children to sharpen their ability to make connections.

Another interesting lesson starter is to begin with an image on the interactive whiteboard which is slowly revealed, and the children have to guess a) what the object is and b) how it might relate to the learning objective for the lesson. Again, this is a way of building those connections, especially connections between the current lesson and those delivered earlier in the week. Similar games can be built around numbers and words.

The odd one out

This game is very well known so I don't claim to be inventing something new here. But I do claim that it is extremely useful for modelling the skill of making new connections, which is fundamental to creativity. As the model learner in the classroom, if the teacher enthuses about it, and introduces it regularly as a lesson starter, then the children will in turn enjoy it and look forward to regular games. This is my experience anyway.

Think of three random objects and ask the children to identify the odd one out. For example:

deckchair   strawberry   table

The obvious answer here is 'strawberry', because it is naturally grown and the other two are man made. Many children will spot this. However, this game becomes especially interesting when you introduce the idea of more than one possible answer – it depends on the connections you choose to make.

For example, one might say that the odd one out is 'table' because the deckchair was red and so is a strawberry. There is nothing say it couldn't be.

Or one might say that the odd one out is 'deckchair' because the other two words contain the letter 'b'.

Or one might choose to argue that 'table' is the odd one out because the other two words both contain smaller words: *deck – chair* and *straw – berry*.

One could go on. What is useful here is the opportunity this game provides for making new connections. And this is exactly what creativity is about.

Let's try it again, because it's enjoyable. Consider the following:

bicycle   fish   rope

One might say that 'bicycle' is the odd one out because the other two do not have wheels but a bicycle does. However, one could also say that 'rope' is the odd one out because the other two move and a rope does not: if the fish were big enough you could ride it, and you can ride a bicycle too. Or one could argue that 'fish' is the odd one out because it is the only living thing. Or perhaps 'rope' is the odd one out because the other two words contain the letter 'i' and rope does not. Or 'bicycle' is the odd one out because the other two words contain just four letters. Or 'fish' is the odd one out because the bicycle was blue and so was the rope, but the fish was orange.

The point of this game is that the children will always be 'correct' if they can justify their answer by showing the connection they have forged. If you can make a connection, then you are right. Can two people who give different answers both be right? Yes, because the links they have made may be equally valid.

The reason why I have such a problem with verbal reasoning tests is because they tend to suggest there is only one 'right' way of making such connections between words, and yet often there are many more. Consequently it shuts down any divergent thinking and promotes convergence towards one acceptable answer. I have often heard colleagues, when introducing a VR test, say to the children, 'Now try not to think about it too much, go with the obvious answer.'

Have you ever heard anything so odd? Why would you require a growing mind *not* to think about something too much and forge a new connection which perhaps the examiner had not thought of? Because it's hard to mark it, that's why.

The odd-one-out game encourages children to do just that – to forge new connections, formulate new answers, and then give an exposition as to why they believe they are correct.

Word games

Another obvious example of making connections is the paired game of 20 questions, where the children have to think of a famous person and their partner must ascertain who he or she is by asking a series of questions, the answer to which can only be 'yes' or 'no'. It does not have to be a famous person, of course.

One can choose an object or a flower or an animal or a country. The questions asked allow the children to sort and classify possibilities, discounting others as they go along because they do not fit with the connection made. As the model learner in the room, you can model how to play the game and, most importantly, highlight how connections can be drawn by asking the most insightful questions. You can show how certain possible answers can be discounted because they do not fit with the information gleaned from the questions asked. This is about connections.

Another suggestion for building connections is the well-known game of citing a word and then the next person must think of a word ending with the last letter of the word before. You can add categories to this – adjectives, or nouns, or names, or colours.

3. Synthesising

As model learner you can influence the degree to which your pupils value creativity by valuing it yourself and sharing your enthusiasm for all things creative. Often the most memorable teacher at school, and the one for which many children will choose to work hard and with whom they enjoy the most positive rapport, will be the teacher who expresses some creativity. This is not to say they will be the art or music teacher necessarily – they may be teaching maths or science or geography – but in some way they will be showing through their actions and words that creativity is important to them.

I recall working alongside a colleague who was a head of maths. Her classroom was adorned with a fine array of colourful plants, pictures and posters and all sorts of displays that were constantly being refreshed. Her creative approach to the subject meant that her pupils looked forward to her lessons. The room was vibrant and colourful and so were the clothes she wore. She enjoyed music too and was forever sharing with the children the latest albums she had purchased (she would invariably sing the songs rather than play them).

Enthusing about any forms of original work is key for the model learner. There follows a few specific examples of how you can share your passion both for your own creative endeavours and for the works of others. In the choices you make, from the music you play, the artwork you display and the books you choose to read to the clothing combinations you wear, you are communicating how much you value originality, whether you know it or not.

Enthuse about reading and telling stories

The teacher who raves about a book they have just enjoyed reading will be inspiring their pupils to read, just as the teacher who enjoys writing and sharing poetry will be encouraging their children to write too. Picture books are my own favourite and they need not be confined to the Key Stage One classroom, by any means. I studied this genre at university and managed a twenty-thousand word dissertation on the uniquely talented Maurice Sendak's *Where the Wild Things Are*. If you have not read it, I heartily recommend it as one of the best picture books ever written. You will have to go a long way to find a better piece of work. Although anything from the super-gifted Oliver Jeffers is stellar too. His *How to Catch a Star* and *Lost and Found* are sublime.

Enthusing about an author's use of language or an illustrator's blend of images will influence the degree to which the children value such creative synthesis.

There are many poetry anthologies too that will help you to share a love of creative writing. *The Rattle Bag* is surely one of the best, along with the staple of most school classrooms, *The Dragon Book of Verse*. For the younger reader, Alan Ahlberg, of course, or Roald Dahl's marvellous *Revolting Rhymes*.

None of these suggestions are especially surprising but this is because they are so good. What is important is to find a piece of creative writing that entertains or moves you, and which you can enthuse about. Reading and enjoying books together in class is such a beneficial practice and encourages the children to begin synthesising their own ideas and experiences into their own stories.

Story making is a practice that makes us human. We are all, by nature, prolific story makers. From the moment we could talk we have, in one way or another, been synthesising words and phrases to tell the story of how we are feeling, what we are thinking and how we wish the world to view us. There is no doubt that every good teacher is a story teller. If Picasso said that we are all born artists and the challenge is to remain an artist as we grow up, then I say all teachers are born story tellers, the challenge is to remain a story teller as the years of teaching take their toll.

It was not only your skills or experience or carefully crafted answers to difficult interview questions that will have you got you the job as a teacher. I am convinced it is because somewhere in the course of the interview you will have revealed that you can tell a good yarn. You can hold an audience and you can enthrall them with the stories you tell.

Narrating the curriculum, telling the story of global knowledge, is what teachers do best. So as model learner you are already modelling storytelling to your pupils.

A good book has suspense, mystery, pace, the element of surprise, and it appeals to the readers' senses. And so too does a lesson. A chapter begins with an exciting hook, plenty of engaging dialogue, some fast-paced action, some multi-sensory engagement and it ends with a cliff-hanger that makes you want to read on.

And so does a lesson.

In the way the teacher reveals the objectives and activities for a lesson, they are modelling the creative process. One might consider one's authorial voice in the same way a writer does. Who is your audience? How will they respond to your style?

The creative gardener

The synthesis of different plant combinations, selected for their colour or form, offers the perfect opportunity for the teacher to demonstrate how much they value creativity. Perhaps you are a keen gardener and can share your enthusiasm and creativity through your choice of indoor plants or by managing a garden outside the classroom if you are lucky enough to have one. Encouraging children to become interested in plants and flowers is an excellent way of instilling a love of creativity, not least because of the endless variety of colours and shapes and designs available to us. It need not involve just pots of pansies and petunias. There are plenty of interesting, architectural plants that will appeal to the more discerning fifteen-year-old boy. The Snake Plant (mother-in-law's tongue) is worth a look, so too the carnivorous Venus Flytrap or the Codariocalyx motorius (Telegraph Plant) which dances, the Snapdragon or the inimitable Sunflower. Orchids are also tremendous plants to grow in classrooms, with fascinating colours, shapes and textures. There are so many intriguing varieties of cactus too. Fortunately none of these plants require great TLC, rather they'd prefer it if you left them to just get on with growing, but they will offer such sensory stimulation for the children.

Sculptures, planned or unplanned

Whether or not you are an accomplished ceramicist, carpenter or sculptor, you can still surround yourself with three dimensional works of art that will hold children's interest and inspire them to be creative. The art teacher in a school is usually grateful for the opportunity to display the work of their many students, space always being limited in the art classroom itself. So there may be a rich source of art pieces at your fingertips in the school, and displaying these around the classroom can help to create a more vibrant, multi-sensory environment.

I remember when I was a class teacher I used to sculpt some weird and wonderful models with my paperclips. It wasn't that I had nothing else to do, you understand, it was because I did it once and the children loved it. So I did it again, and again, until eventually I would arrive extra early just so that I could fashion some new piece of sculpture which the children would delight in when they trudged sleepily and moodily into the classroom on a rainy morning. It was quirky and fun and refreshingly nothing to do with the curriculum or learning objectives for the day.

But what this paperclip sculpting did do was inject a little sense of drama into the classroom, a sense of anticipation – what would they expect to find that morning? A giant walking man, a ship, a failed attempt at a go-kart or perhaps a miniature climbing frame. I did the same thing with rubber bands and pencils, of which there are usually endless supplies in most classrooms. I constructed a variety of sculptures, some of them recognisable objects like houses, shelters and chairs, others entirely open to interpretation (because my original designs went wrong).

The model learner should share their infectious enthusiasm for creating, whether it is improvised concoctions made of pens and elastic bands or accomplished works of art. The important thing is to keep creating and adorning one's classroom with pieces that will intrigue.

Improvisation

Improvisation is very much about drawing on one's experience, using one's perception and then making new connections – and quickly. This is such good practice for the creative mind.

Of course, when one says 'improvisation' one often thinks of brave actors and actresses on a stage doing wacky things with words and body language on demand. This is not what I mean, though it is wonderful fun, of course, and very good for creativity. *Whose line is it anyway?* was a very popular television show and it was always so impressive to see how quick-witted and sharp the participants were, able to create fictional characters, scenarios and dialogue from nothing but a word or theme provided to them three seconds before. The ability to perform spontaneously and with a vivid imagination is a key skill for the creative person but this is only one very specific example of being creative – and improvisation of this kind may fill not only some students with fear and dread but their teachers too. Making connections and thinking creatively on demand, and in a public arena, will surely test the bravest of performers.

I am talking about other kinds of improvisational activities. Those moments when we feel uninhibited and free to make connections that others may not have considered. When we are provided with a mix of ingredients and prompts and we see things which others may not. As model learner we can demonstrate this in so many ways.

A favourite for many teachers is hot-seating, in which pupils in the role of characters from books read, films watched or plays enacted together take turns to sit in the chair at the front of the classroom and field questions from the rest of the class. This is a highly creative activity, not only for the person in the hot seat but so too for the rest of the class, who are using their imagination to project a different role and personality on to the person in the hot seat and suspend their disbelief to be able to ask questions of that character, as if they were really there.

When 'choosing volunteers' to take a turn in the hot seat, I would invariably ask them to step outside first of all so I could brief them on who they were going to be. On returning to the classroom I would usually say, 'Waiting outside is a very special guest who I'm sure we all can't wait to meet.' Once the interview had concluded, the person would step outside again and then return as themselves, citing they had just been to a music lesson. I would, of course, tell them it was pity that they had just missed a special visitor. 'You'll never guess who just visited while you were out!'

'Mantle of the Expert'

I studied the work of the great Dorothy Heathcote whilst at university and I have been an admirer of hers, and an advocate of her practices, ever since. Lauded as 'one of the greatest teachers of the twentieth century', Heathcote promoted an approach that places the child at the centre of the learning. All planning for learning is 'wrapped around the child' from the planning stage, hence the word *mantle*. The child is enveloped in the qualities of leadership, enquiry, knowledge and understanding and a 'fictional expertise'. In Mantle of the Expert activities, the children are invited to imagine themselves in the role of expert – from scientist to journalist to archeologist or sales and marketing executive, and complete a project or task set for them.

As Heathcote always advocated, the teacher is very much in the drama too – modelling for the children how to suspend their disbelief and 'join in'.

This is most relevant to our cause here, since modelling creativity means communicating to the children, through our actions, that it is indeed worth participating in something imaginative, worth suspending one's disbelief and having a go. Heathcote's teacher-in-role approach is central if we are to encourage children to engage in creative play, as we actively serve as an example to them. 'If the teacher believes in this then perhaps it is worth doing.' I will return to Mantle of the Expert and group role play in the following chapter on group dynamics. For now, dramatic approaches to learning can really engage pupils' interest and deepen their understanding of a topic, situation or concept – and as model learner we serve the children best when we plunge into the drama and believe in it.

Dramatic activities might include:

- a marketing team charged with the task of promoting a new book
- a team of archeologists presented with a new find in the playground
- a group of town planners deciding on the merits of an application to build a new supermarket in a suburb out of town

- a team of event managers, charged with the task of hosting an arts festival
- a group of nutritionists, asked to design a new weekly menu for the school
- a local tourist board asked to design anew campaign to attract new visitors
- a group of film-makers asked to create a short film to promote the school

These tasks require the children to perceive and understand the problem or challenge presented to them, make connections and then synthesise their ideas to find creative solutions and deliver results.

4. Presenting

This fourth stage of the creative process is, by the very nature of what teachers do, the most frequently modelled one. We are, after all, lead presenter for the curriculum we teach and the key storyteller in the room. It's not just what we say, it's the way we say it.

Teachers are such skilled presenters, exhibiting all the necessary skills one needs to be an effective communicator and honing these skills every day in the classroom. I have often believed that public speaking is not difficult if you have something to say – some nugget of information you are keen to impart and which you can enthuse about. But this book is about creativity particularly and how this fourth stage is crucial to the creative process. We are looking to build in those 'ta-dah moments' as much as possible, because they drive our creativity, giving us an opportunity to share what we have done and take pride in it, and because they provide a deadline, a target to work towards.

The fun I had with those buttons was made extra special because I knew there was an appreciative audience at the end of the process. My Nana was always going to cherish what I had created for her – and I probably knew that – but it still seemed special when her face lit up with delight and she shared words of encouragement at a finished piece of button artwork or sculpture. So believing in the children's creativity is key. Appreciative words of encouragement during the 'ta-dah moment' go a long way.

I believe in the 'show and tell' aspect of teaching and learning. Every child must feel that there will be a time for them to show what they have created, and that their efforts matter and are valued. As model learners we can demonstrate how to respond to the creative work of others when they show it and tell us about it. We can demonstrate to the children how we must respect and value what others have done, even if we think we can do better. Though I have already said that the intrinsic motivation to create is what matters – rather than the motivation to impress others when we exhibit what we've done – there is still great excitement to be found in sharing our creations and receiving recognition for them.

Children may not always be the first to praise another's child's creations. It is down to us as teachers to do that and to invite others to agree with us that what has been created is impressive! Setting the tone for a celebration of creative talent is very much what good teaching and learning are about. We can model for the children how to respond to work that is relatively good for the creator's own ability. This is central to the presentation stage.

When creative work is presented to the class, and to us, it is important that there are no preconceived ideas as to what constitutes good or bad, pass or fail. That is to say, although there is much in school which is marked against standardised norms and expectations, creative work is subjective and can be valued against quite different criteria. By its nature, each creation will be unique, one hopes, and so the criteria for assessing it will be different and inextricably linked to the creator's own expectations and plans. One might consider, for example, how much the finished product matches the intended design envisaged by the creator. Is it what they had hoped it would be? Could they improve on it? Does the design fit the need or purpose? Have the creative skills involved been employed successfully, or could something be honed and improved and refined?

When children present their creative work to the teacher, or parent, very often the first question might be, 'Are you proud of it?' This, I think, is key. In many ways, the 'show and tell' is to the creator himself. In preparing the product ready for exhibition to the class, the creator is preparing it for his own critique. Only then will he step back and consider its merits. And that is precisely the moment when the teacher's input is crucial, because there are many, many children who will not rate their own work as highly as they should.

Many readers will recognise the child who, when asked what they think of their finished picture or story or musical composition will mumble 'S'ok, s'pose.' There is always the possibility of some false modesty here, especially if the question is posed in front of peers, but the inability to give oneself full credit when critiquing one's own work is present in all of us, I believe. It's an insurance policy; better to be self-effacing and modest than to say we think it's brilliant, we're very proud of it and then risk facing the appalling prospect of others disagreeing. The teacher is the interlocutor: the go-between who gives the young creator licence to be proud and positive about what they have done, even in front of others.

Planning for 'show and tell' sessions and considering carefully how we present, and how we respond to others', creative work is especially important in a school environment because so much of what children produce in school is ordinarily shown and told through grades. Whether we like it or not, much of what the children work on, no matter how creatively they do so, will ultimately end up with a grade attached to it and this is as far from a 'ta-dah moment' as you can possibly get. There is no dialogue, no narration, no exposition from the creator, talking us through their mental and creative processes. Write a good story in an English exam and all you get back is a grade. It is only through creative classwork that children are afforded time to present and narrate what they have created. And that matters.

Of course, it would be wrong to say that all children look forward to showing and telling their work, or performing creatively in front of others. They don't. For many, this fourth stage is purgatory. But as model learner we can emphasise the benefits of presenting and performing. Sharing our creative talent is good for us and it spurs us on to create again. The warm glow of pride one derives from performing in assembly, on a drama stage or in a concert, especially when it goes well, is always worth the time, effort and nervous energy invested. We can demonstrate this to the children by readily performing or presenting ourselves, through delivering assemblies, participating in school plays and concerts, and just by presenting the lessons in class every day.

Not only does the presentation stage give the creator something to aim for, as mentioned earlier, it also gives the creator renewed self-confidence and optimism when the presentation is well received (which it must always be in school). It can be an energising, restorative experience and can set in motion renewed determination to create, and then present, again and again. Creativity does not depend on presentation in order to survive – there are many secret artists and musicians who are prolific in their output but choose not to share their works, I am sure – but presentation can inspire others to create, and that in itself can be hugely rewarding for the presenter.

4 The Language of Learning

As with all attitudes and aptitudes that make up the invisible curriculum, the language we use to comment on *creativity* in school can have a profound effect on its survival. The way we comment on the children's 'invisible ink' can have the effects of diminishing it or encouraging it to flourish, depending on the words we choose to use, and creativity is no exception to this.

Let me give you an example. In Book 1 I discussed how the word 'progress' suggests advancement towards a pre-ordained destination. How else can you measure a child's progress unless you know where they have come from and where they are supposed to be heading? But what is this destination exactly where creativity is concerned? We can set targets for developing creative skills, such as technical drawing skills in art, creative writing skills or musical composition skills and we can assess the extent to which a child has demonstrated a mastery of these skills – this is achievable; but how can we judge whether a child has made 'progress' in terms of their imagination, their self-motivation, their sensory perception, their ability to make connections or their enthusiasm for sharing what they have created? There are so many variables at play here, so many contributing factors that lie behind the visible skills we see being displayed, all of which are essential for creativity to survive.

As I said earlier, Somerset Maugham believed that writers write not because they want to but because they *have to*. So how do you assess whether a child's innate compulsion to write has progressed? How do you measure their keenness?

Just as we cannot fatten a pig by weighing it, so children will not become keener to create by having their keenness measured. But you can comment on the pupils' inclination to create, provided you use language that conveys a growth mindset, or a potential mindset, rather than a fixed one. You can inspire creativity and provide a useful commentary on it too if you look beyond the usual language of assessment, such as these unhelpful words like *progress* or *results*. Save those for the literacy and numeracy lessons or the VR and NVR tests. Creativity requires a different lexicon.

When encouraging the children to engage in creative activity, it is worth considering the language we use to talk about sensory perception, since this is the first stage in the creative process.

We have looked earlier at our senses and the nomenclature of those many other senses that scientists are now suggesting we have – thermoception, nociception and so on. It is worth exploring those other senses and the terminology involved. This is not because children need to be tested on which sense has which technical name; rather it is because knowing there is a separate name for something allows us to appreciate it exists – this is how we humans are built, I believe. We have a fascination for naming things. Only then do we seem to accept it exists. What is that called? What does this mean? What is it similar too? Pondering these sorts of questions is what makes us human.

Once you have considered the names of our myriad senses, you may wish to encourage the children to 'eat a thesaurus'. An extended vocabulary helps us to articulate our emotional responses to sensory experiences. There would have been no point in taking the children down to the cellars of the school to look at cobwebs and soak up the atmosphere if their responses had been confined to 'it was amazing' or 'like, cool, yeah.' I may be getting old, but the word 'amazing' does seem to crop up more frequently than ever these days and it seems such a shame that it is used as a one-size-fits-all for just about anything that has a positive impact on our senses.

Creativity is greatly aided by an ability to feel emotions in response to stimuli around us and when we can articulate those emotions in words other than 'amazing', both to ourselves and to others, then we can start to connect and synthesise, and create something original. So it is always worth broadening children's vocabulary within a particular creative discipline, whether it is articulating a response to a musical stimuli, or a sensory experience outside that is turned into poetic lines.

Using language to make associations one wouldn't normally make is an interesting exercise too. For example, one might play a piece of music and ask the children to describe what colour it is. Or describe in words what shape Monday is, or what jealousy would feel like if you could touch it. Or share a flower and consider what its voice might sound like if it could talk.

The benefit of such activities is that they actively encourage unique responses, there can be no correct one and therefore no incorrect one. Each response given makes sense to the person articulating it, but they too can appreciate how others may see things differently. These activities are encouraging the children to search for new words and phrases to express their imaginative ideas.

The idea of valuing everyone's ideas is central to encouraging creativity in school. In this regard, rather than asking who has the best idea, ask who has the *most* ideas. Or begin with the answer and invite the children to come up with a plausible question to match it.

Creativity is an activity which occurs in school and that means it is vulnerable to the language used for monitoring, evaluating and reporting on most activity in school – the language of assessment: the adjectives and nouns associated with progress, the numerical and letter grades to indicate levels, the summative reports, and the shorthand ways we have of recognising effort – the ubiquitous burnt steaks (well done).

But one can and should use language to comment on the children's creative behaviours. The following words can be used to describe the children's efforts in each of the four stages of creativity, and these words give us a guide to the kind of creative behaviours we are looking for in the children.

Creative stage	Language to describe behaviour
Perceiving	perceptive, inquisitive, observant, alert, switched-on, sensitive, empathetic, watchful, curious, interested
Connecting	innovative, inventive, intuitive, instinctive, understanding, thoughtful, objective, independent
Synthesising	creative, resourceful, imaginative, skillful, committed, resilient, determined, disciplined, meticulous, careful, thorough
Presenting	communicative, articulate, detailed, open, expressive, knowledgeable, conversant, animated, trusting

Have a wide lexicon of words of phrases with which we can comment on the children's creative behaviour seems sensible to me, and allows us to provide a commentary without influencing the creative process with our judgements. But these words describe the process not the product, of course. There must come a time when some kind of value is placed on the children's creations – they will expect it and so will their parents. Here, the language we use will be of supreme importance, since 'marking' a child's creative work may hold such influence over that child's future desire to create again, her intrinsic motivation.

Marking creative work

Whenever we mark children's work we will always give an impression that there is a set of success criteria and a scale of marks available. Often, in some subjects this is absolutely correct. The success criteria may have been laid down at the beginning of the lesson, in the form of learning objectives, or it may have been modelled by the teacher – *ie* they demonstrate 'how to do' something, whether it is a multiplication sum, the use of direct speech, or simple science experiment. There is a clear 'way of doing things' and if the children follow this way then they are going to earn good marks.

We need to draw a distinction here between skills and imagination. There may well be a particular way of using a paintbrush effectively, or playing a musical instrument or holding a fountain pen. Clearly these ways can be modelled by the teacher – and the degree to which the child has mastered these skills can be monitored and commented upon in the usual way. But what of the imagination needed in order to create something new with those skills? How do we comment on that? How do we mark something not only for the skills deployed and demonstrated whilst creating it – which, arguably, can be marked – but also for the originality of thought that went into it, the imagination that led to its creation at all. How do we mark that?

There are two criteria here which will help us: the creator's original intentions and the originality of outcome. Has the creative product matched up to what its creator wanted and was envisioning? And does the product have an original element to it? Is there evidence of something new here?

Let's take the first criterion, the question of whether the creative product lived up to the creator's expectations. Has it delivered on what he was envisaging? The only ways we can know this are by talking to the creator himself and considering his aims for the project. This is where the presentation stage comes in.

We cannot hope to give the young creator a mark for his work before we have listened to his presentation of that work, which will hopefully contain a commentary on how successful it has been in satisfying his own intentions and design brief. He will know if it is any good. He will know if it has delivered on what was in his mind when he embarked on the creative project. The images in his head, which so tantalisingly drove him on to create will be very real for him and they will be the benchmark against which he will mark the final outcome. It is a brutal process and one which we, as teachers, may need to protect him from. We always have an idea of how splendid our creative work is going to look and it is rare for the real thing to match up, isn't it. Some careful diplomacy may be needed here, as we encourage the creator to see beyond the tiny flaws and see the bigger picture. But part of being creative is being a perfectionist. When the creative impulse strikes and we begin creating, we very often will settle for nothing less than perfection. So when the product is 'finished' (if it is ever finished) it is likely we will notice the flaws and imperfections more readily than we will notice the successful aspects of the piece.

Notwithstanding the little imperfections then, we can encourage the creator to tell us whether it lived up to what he was intending it to be. In this respect, the following questions may be useful to us:

● Has the product matched up to your expectations for it?

● Does it resemble what was in your mind at the beginning of this?

● Are you proud of what you have created? What are you most proud of? What are you least proud of?

● How could you make this better next time? What would you do differently?

Secondly, we can address the uniqueness of the piece. Does it contain an element of originality or is it completely derivative? Naturally, in school, where we are modelling creative processes and the children are mimicking them, there will be much that is unoriginal in the work produced, but there will also be an element of the child himself, something that makes the work different to anyone else's. And the child may be blind to this, because they are too close to it, of course. But what is crucial here is the way in which we deliver our commentary or judgement.

We can use language that emphasises originality as well as quality. That is not to say any old scratch on a piece of paper can be rated as highly creative and therefore worthy of a good mark. There needs to be a structure, a process employed, a design brief which has been delivered on, a plan, an idea articulated, a vision which has been turned into a reality – none of these things can really be articulated through a scruffy mark on a page. So I am not advocating originality *over* quality, and that we should just give children a box of coloured pencils and say 'find your inner creator' and then marvel at the abstract markings they've experimentally scribbled on the page with one hand whilst picking their nose with the other. I think it's banal to say that anything is creative, just because it's been created. I am all for improvisation, and this has tremendous value, but we are talking about the deliberate and careful creativity in school which leads to a child presenting their original work to the class. This is far from giving them free reign. It is helping them to have a creative vision, to turn that into a reality and then to be able to articulate and present that vision to an audience.

And in this respect, originality is absolutely key. Can that child show evidence of some original thought – their choice of setting or character in a story written, their use of colour or technique in a drawing, the blend of notes they have synthesised in a musical composition, or their innovative thinking that creates a novel solution in a problem-solving exercise. Have they written, or painted or played or thought something which no one else has before them, in that particular way? If they have, then the product can be judged to be creative.

In this respect, the following sentence starters may be useful when we attempt to 'mark' what they have done. In each case, the comments very deliberately emphasise the child's own efforts, placing them in ownership of actions and decisions taken during the creative process.

- Your decision to use…
- Your selection of ….
- I like the way you have chosen to use…
- Your use of…
- Your choice of…
- You have managed to…

- You have delivered on…

- This shows you have thought about…

- The connections you have made…

- You have thought about…

- You have used your imagination to…

Placing the child's decision-making and independent actions at the centre of the marking process is key if we are to empower and encourage them to create again. We must remind them that it is their work, their efforts, their decisions. And that they can do it again next time, even better perhaps.

The problem with a lot of marking is that it offers a grade which indicates how closely (or not) the children's work has matched up to 'what we are looking for'. I have never liked that old inspector of children's work, WILF, and his cousin WALT. Which of our pupils are actually motivated by the phrase 'We Are Learning To…' or, even worse, by 'What I'm Looking For…'?

Together, Walt and Wilf remind me of the old boys, Statler and Waldorf, who used to sit in the box at the Muppet Show theatre and heckle, offering miserable critiques to all and sundry. They could never be pleased. We all remember teachers like Statler and Waldorf, don't we. Those for whom the criteria for any work we did in class was simply how closely it matched their own expectations, or in some case how closely it mimicked the 'control' they modelled at the beginning of the lesson for us.

Our critiques of the children's creative endeavours need to be very positive and emphasise at every moment the decisions the children have made along the way, placing them in control so they don't feel disempowered or disinterested next time.

In a tremendous work of fiction by David Klass, called *You don't know me*, the author offers a most accurate view of how some pupils see the question of ownership of work in school. The protagonist, a teenage student with a lot going on in his life, says that the homework he has been set by his maths teacher is not, in any way, *his* work, because the teacher has set it and she will be marking it, so it's *her* work. I have some sympathy with this view. And, when it comes to creativity, such a response can be very demotivating for the young creator. Ownership is key.

The language we use to critique the children's creative work must therefore move ownership from the teacher who set the work to the child who completes it. As the DfE's Teachers' Standards state, we must 'encourage pupils to take a responsible and conscientious attitude to their own work and study.'

Another facet of the language we use to encourage and then comment on the children's creativity is that it needs to reduce the element of extrinsic rewards and competition. I don't believe children, or anyone for that matter, indulges in creative activity in order to win accolades and beat everyone else. If creators do harbor these ambitions I suspect that their creativity will wane pretty quickly. The creator creates because they have to – there will have been a creative impulse that needs satisfying. The moment extrinsic rewards and accolades are mentioned, some creators may find that their intrinsic motivation to go on creating is stymied.

This is not to say that we must therefore never award cups and prizes and certificates to creative children for the wonderful pieces they have made. Clearly this would be an odd thing to do, but in celebrating the children's creative endeavours, we would be wise to continually flag up the benefits and pleasures such creativity has brought the children *themselves* – how proud they feel of their efforts, how much they have learned and how they will be able to do even better next time. This is different to saying they must be proud of the accolades they have won, or for being mentioned in assembly or having their poem feature in a school newsletter.

The greatest reward for a creator is for the sense of achievement they feel when they have managed to turn a vision into a reality. They have brought something into the world that did not exist before, only in their head. External rewards and praise may follow as a result of this, but they are happy by-products only, they were not the reasons for creating in the first place.

When we move around the classroom, chivvying the children on to continue with their drawings or stories or musical compositions, we must be so very careful that we consider the impact our words will have not only on the intended recipient of them, but on the others in the vicinity.

I have seen teachers hover over desks and hand out motivational compliments such as, 'Wow, that's great, David, keep going!' or 'Very good, Molly. Really super!' and David and Molly feel good. But what about Jonathan sitting next to

David? Or Lisa who shares Molly's table? What do you say to them? Unless you give out a compliment which has exactly the same value as those given to David and Molly, then the intrinsic motivation inside Jonathan and Lisa will diminish, surely.

But what is the alternative? Do we keep quiet and just let them create? Or do we move around the tables and give the same praise to every individual, just slightly reworded?

I think the answer is the latter. We do indeed praise and motivate each individual child – because, as teachers, we have a wide lexicon of motivational phrases which we can blend together in a myriad different ways. It's our job, it's what we do. We find something about the work we like or, even better, something about the effort the child is showing. After all, it is only the effort they can change. Praising a child for being creative is as useful as praising a child for being tall. There's nothing they can do about that. What they can change is their *effort*. So we focus as much as possible on the efforts the children are showing in the creative lesson. The child who is working hard and concentrating and absorbed and 'in a flow state' as we often say today, is the child who will create something truly special. So we focus on that.

But to achieve a 'flow state', when we feel truly absorbed in the creative process, requires one to be free of distraction. So moving around the room to give out praise should be kept to a minimum so as not to disturb the creative flow! It reminds me of the keen and helpful waiter who attends your table, just as you are filling your mouth with delicious food, to watch you eating and ask, 'Is everything okay with your food?' It's terribly intrusive, isn't it, especially when you know only because it's company policy to insist that the waiting staff must ask the patrons if everything is okay two minutes after the food has arrived. I'm sure they wait until you have filled your mouth before attending, so all you can do is a submissive nod of the head, or they wait until you are regaling your guests with an anecdote or joke and spring up just moments from the punchline.

Leave them to it, I say.

5 Group dynamics

When delivering CPD in schools on the subject of creativity, I have often asked the staff to draw something. I hand out paper and pencils and then invite everyone in the room to produce their own sketch of a horse. Is there a more difficult animal to draw?

It is a fascinating activity. What is clear, after only the first minute, is that the teachers' own artistic ability to draw a horse is by no means their only concern. There are so many other factors at play, all of which influence greatly the outcome. There is the person's own optimism that what they will draw will not resemble a three-legged, hump-backed donkey. Without optimism and self-belief they will wriggle and make excuses and pay a conveniently-timed trip to the toilet – anything to avoid putting pencil to paper. Unless they think they can do it properly, often they won't even start it.

Then there is the overwhelming concern that the horse one draws will not be as good – or anywhere near as good – as the horse drawn by the da Vinci sitting next to them. Oh, the crushing embarrassment when you find you're far less able than your neighbour!

Then there is the concern that I, as teacher, will be coming around the tables. Which I do, of course, peering over everyone's shoulders and offering words of encouragement. I always choose two people sitting next to each other and say to the first, 'Great, brilliant, that's looking excellent.' And then to the second, 'Okay, keep going.' The result is always guffawing and sympathetic nods of the head when we realise the impact our words have on the pupils and their neighbours (see previous chapter).

Then there is the concern that the horse they draw is not what I, as teacher and therefore the person who is 'always right', will be expecting. Will their horse be different to the one I have 'made earlier' and am about to reveal to them in spectacular celebration of my own artistic talents? Will theirs be as good as mine?

And, of course, there is the very real worry that their horse *will* be good enough and will therefore be held up to their colleagues as an example of how to do it. Oh, the crushing embarrassment when you find you're far more able than your neighbours!

It is often hard to see how our innate creative talents can ever flourish in this group setting, and yet we require children to express themselves creatively in a group situation all the time. We set them a writing task or a painting task or perhaps some creative thinking challenge and then we expect them to just get on with it, oblivious to the fact that everyone around them is creating too, and that they may very well be judged against others' efforts when the lesson reaches its conclusion in a glorious show and tell.

It is tempting at this juncture to give up being creative in school altogether and recommend that any form of creative activity is confined to the privacy of one's home, or relative privacy. But there is much that can and should be taught about creativity in the school setting; the key is to link it to *effort* rather than *talent*. As I have alluded to earlier, telling a child she is talented is about as useful as telling her she is tall. There is nothing you can do about that, but what you can change is the amount of effort she puts in, so it is worth focusing on that. The creative classroom promulgates the growth mindset – that we can all improve by putting in more effort. There is no fixed ceiling to our creative talents because there is no limit to the effort we can put in. There isn't a single child who cannot produce something because every child is unique! But to get better we need to invest more effort and energy and passion into what we're doing – and no one is precluded from doing that, we can all do it.

The most effective creative classroom is one in which everyone feels a sense of being in it together and mutual respect abounds. Indeed, the DfE's Teachers' Standards require us to 'establish a safe and stimulating environment for pupils, rooted in mutual respect.'

We are all in the same boat. But like any organisation, a class needs shared values if its students are to feel happy and comfortable enough to express their creativity – an activity fraught with so many worries, as the drawing of the horse shows.

It may be worth considering some creative values which you can keep returning to prior to setting creative tasks. My suggestions are:

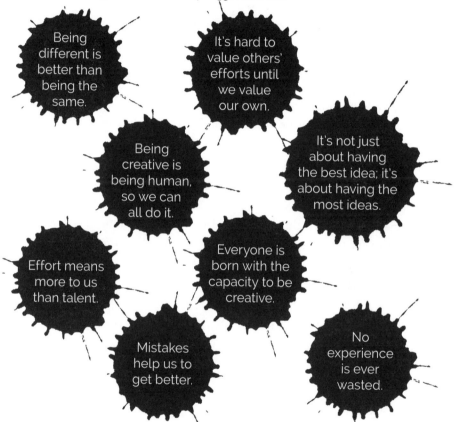

Being different is better than being the same.

It's hard to value others' efforts until we value our own.

Being creative is being human, so we can all do it.

It's not just about having the best idea; it's about having the most ideas.

Effort means more to us than talent.

Everyone is born with the capacity to be creative.

Mistakes help us to get better.

No experience is ever wasted.

Producing a display of shared values such as these is an effective way of providing real evidence that you are meeting a number of DfE's Teachers' Standards, and especially: 'have a secure understanding of how a range of factors can inhibit pupils' ability to lean, and how best to overcome these.' By publishing shared values you are recognising that you understand how many children can feel inhibited by the group dynamics of the classroom, and that you are making efforts to address this.

Regularly revisiting such shared values in class will help each pupil to place trust in the group – and trust is everything when it comes to expressing one's creativity in front of others. We need to know that our own creative endeavours will be valued for what they are; we need to feel confident that it is indeed worth having a go, despite the risk of failing and looking foolish. In the creative classroom any effort is rewarded, any willingness to have a go and risk sharing your creative thoughts with the group is always appreciated.

We cannot expect the children's creativity to flourish unless we address the social context in which they are creating – and that means reinforcing an equitable and supportive environment, in which behaviour is as closely monitored as attainment. Any form of work is affected by the context in which it occurs, and the people along side you are working, but this is especially true of creative work – precisely because you are giving something extra of yourself. You are revealing your imagination, your ambitions and your plans – right in front of other people.

I visit schools regularly to advise on creativity in the curriculum. I often visit creative classrooms where the children are all busy getting on with something imaginative – whether it's writing, problem-solving, designing, performing or some other creative pursuit. The children are all expressing themselves right next to one another, in a crowd. Where it is done successfully, and everyone is happy to commit to their creative ambitions and have a go, it is where the children are encouraged to support one another and no one is overtly competing.

Of course, if the creative task is engrossing enough and the children are 'hooked' then the group dynamic quickly fades into the background and the children become absorbed in what they are doing. But getting started is the hardest part of all and for any young creator to dare to set foot on the creative path in a public arena like a classroom, then they need to know it is safe to do so.

Celebrating difference

A culture that celebrates individuality and rejects conformity is always going to be a tricky one to establish in a school. Let's face it, much of school life requires the children to conform – they wear a uniform, they sit in rows, they listen when they're spoken to, they arrive and depart lessons when the bell strikes and they all work next to one another like cows in a milking shed. But if this all seems wholly conforming on the surface, it is in the relationships we enjoy with our students and the discourse of the classroom in which creativity is given licence. There is a rich variety in every classroom and we can celebrate this: we have different names, different appearances, different likes and dislikes, different hopes and dreams, different worries and phobias and different stories to tell about our families, our homes and the lives we are playing out each day. There are so many ways to recognise this in school, from those wonderfully individualised labels and pegs hanging up the coats, to the name tags for drawers and lockers or the individual pencil cases that furnish every school desk. There are the hair cuts, the shoes, the spectacles, the jewellery (if it's allowed), the phone cases and the school bags.

Wherever individual expression is allowed, it is worth us talking to the children about it and showing that we have noticed them for who they are. Using children's names, for example, when we speak to them, reinforces this notion that it is ok to be Jonathan at school – that there is a Jonathan-shaped space at that school for him, and there will always be one for as long as he is there.

I have often heard parents and teachers talk about how we must not 'round off the corners' of our children in the rush to push them through the various and necessary hoops and obstacles of the examination system. But parents needn't worry too much – every teacher I've met has always celebrated the little idiosyncrasies of their pupils, it's what make teaching them so much fun (and such a challenge!). But how often do we communicate this to the children? How often do we remind them that it's okay to be themselves? How often do we remind them that there is indeed room for them in our classrooms. The idea that we all have to conform to some stereotypical model of a pupil is a myth, peddled by onlookers who have never taught a class of children in their lives, or by teachers who are reluctant to go that extra mile and unleash the children's creativity either because they are afraid of the consequences or because they just can't be bothered. Blaming 'the system' for promoting a conformist approach in which individuals' needs are ignored is an excuse for poor teaching, I believe. The DfE's Teachers' Standards require us to 'manage classes effectively, using approaches which are appropriate to pupils' needs in order to involve and motivate them.'

So it is clear that every teacher is not only encouraged, but required, to address individual children's needs and find ways to motivate every pupil they teach. This means going that extra mile to encourage the children to be themselves – and that is good news for creativity, since it has originality at its heart.

6 Choices and challenges

Rooted in the creative process is the idea of *freedom*: freedom to explore and discover, to experiment and try things out for the first time, freedom to make mistakes and learn from them, to improvise and dare to have a go. There is nothing so demotivating than to be set a narrowly defined task, the criteria for which has been pre-ordained (back to our friends Walt and Wilf again) and the resources for which have already been found and presented. There is little room here for the kind of experimentation and discovery that young creators need to stay motivated.

As Stein (1984) argues:

> Creative persons need the freedom for study and preparation, the freedom for exploration and enquiry, the freedom of expression and the freedom to be themselves. (Stein, 1984: 18)

There must exist some element of choice within the brief given – whether this is in the choice of materials and resources used, or in the way a problem is tackled or a design brief is met.

Of course, it is precisely in the open-ended nature of creative lessons where some teachers may harbor reservations because all this 'freedom' and element of choice can lead to arguments when instructions are not spelled out with timescale and deadlines printed indelibly on the board. Give them some freedom to make choices and some children may spend longer deciding than doing, finding any excuse they can to prevaricate and quibble – anything but get on with it. That's the risk we take. And no-one is suggesting that the child who cannot decide on how he is going to approach a creative task cannot receive some guidance, or some coercion to get a move on and choose.

Independent projects that involve some element of choice and ownership will always be good for creativity. All subjects in the curriculum lend themselves to independent projects in one way or another, whether it is a geography research project, a history presentation, a maths problem-solving activity or a group drama.

Returning to my Nana's button box for a moment, one of the reasons why I felt so enamoured with it was because of the free reign I enjoyed when playing with those buttons. Had my Nana told me that this week she would like a blue necklace, and next week she would like a bracelet made only of white buttons, I suspect my motivation to create would have waned very quickly. She didn't know what I was going to make from one week to the next, and the really exciting thing was neither did I.

Twenty-five years later, when my son Henry returned from visiting HMS Victory I did not tell him that I wanted a five-page book on Admiral Nelson, with four pictures, five hundred words and accurate use of time connectives. It was his work, his creation. What I had done was provide the conditions in which the creative impulse was born. I immersed Henry in a sensory adventure, after which he had little choice but to create, create, create because he felt the need to give vent to the thoughts and emotional responses buzzing around his head. The shape and format of those thoughts was, to a great extent, left up to him.

But clearly such free liberty cannot always be achievable in a school setting, where there is a curriculum to be taught and learned, examinations to be passed, and progress and improvement to be measured. Of course teachers must set the work and then mark it. But there is room, I hope, to offer the children some independent projects in which they may exercise some choice over how content is accessed and collated, how thoughts are articulated and original ideas are synthesised, and how their work is presented at the end.

It is hard to see children's innate creativity in action when these choices are removed entirely from their range and work is set within very tight parameters. (I've often wondered why homework set in school should have to be handed in the very next morning. Surely one of the very few benefits of setting homework at all is to encourage children to manage their time and choose when they do it, provided it is done before the deadline of a week or two?).

I wonder how much work in class actually consists of nothing more than the receiving, analysing and presenting of data? We provide established, propositional information, they receive it, analyse it and write essays on it to show they have understood it. Where is the creativity in this?

But then so much of the world today involves data collection and analysis, and that's it. The extraordinary growth of computer technology has influenced the way we live our lives and the pace at which we live them. 'Here is some information, you need to process it and respond as quickly as you can to it. Quick, hurry up.'

It's called an email. Or a text. And our lives seem to be plagued by them. Instant information, requiring an instant response, with little or almost no room for creativity.

But if we spend so much of our lives receiving, analysing and responding to information, surely human progress will eventually halt, won't it? If so many of us spend so much of our lives shuffling data around and responding to it with much of the same kind of data, who is coming up with the new ideas?

School must be one such place where the habit of slavishly peddling banal information around is stopped – and we make space and time for the children to think, speak and write new thoughts.

We have a choice every time we communicate, if you think about it. Should we reach for new ways of expressing how we feel, or shall we settle for the usual phrases which serve just as well? If someone asks, 'How are you?' the chances are you will think about it for a very brief moment and then answer in the usual fashion, 'Fine, thanks,' or 'Okay' or 'Alright, thanks, how're you?' That's probably all the questioner wanted to hear, anyway.

Nothing surprising there. But scale this up to every aspect of communication in your life and you may see a worrying preference for nothing out of the ordinary! Emails, phone calls, television programmes, hobbies, work routines, eating habits, and friendships – we are all predisposed to patterns. Habits of mind. Few of those habits are innovative, many of them are entirely uncreative because they are done on 'auto pilot'. They are what we are comfortable with, and it's how our brains are built. Our survival instinct doesn't like the unexpected so we surround ourselves with the expected.

'What do you want from the Chinese takeaway, the usual?'

'What are you drinking? The usual?'

'Daily Mail, as usual?'

'It's been a great holiday, same place next year?'

'Nice meal, can we have that again please?'

'These shoes are great, I should have bought a spare pair.'

None of these choices are made because they are right or they are daringly wrong, but just because they are habits. They are familiar to us so we do them again and again. They hold no threat the first time so we can be safe with them the next time – we have removed one more threatening situation from our lives, so the survival function of our old, animal brain is entirely happy.

If creativity is about doing something new and original then how do we know it will make us happier? It may not! If it involves 'thinking outside the box' then how on earth can we be sure we'll be safe outside the box? Surely it's safer inside it, isn't it?

Interestingly, the aspects of humans that make us more advanced as a species than any other in the history of the planet have very little to do with the survival part of our brains, rather it has everything to do with ignoring this part.

In young children the creative thinking part of the brain is yet to fully form and so the survival part of the brain is very much 'in charge'. It is our job as teachers to gently coax children out of this dominant, ruling pattern and into new experiences that will prompt new ways of thinking and doing and behaving. If we remove the need for children to make independent choices, their survival brain may be quite content with this, because we have organised their lives for them and, as responsible adults, they can safely assume that we have their health and best interests at heart. Job done. Progress halted and future potential missed.

We must provide children with the opportunities to choose to be different, choose to try something new, even just once, and then revert back again to something more familiar again if they need to.

Have you ever tried to encourage your young child to eat a new type of vegetable? Or stroke an animal they've not encountered before, or put their hand into a fish tank, or sleep with the light off? They have an overwhelming fear of the unknown, or most young children do, though not all, of course. They have a very strong sense of self-preservation and this limits their courage and willingness to try new things – especially sprouts.

We need to present children with choices and then give them the chance to see the benefits to be found in choosing the less obvious, less comfortable pathways. This is how we build that creative spirit in all of us – that sense of adventure. There is a great sense of accomplishment to be found in choosing the less familiar, more daring option and then discovering that we enjoyed it and found success there.

Facing challenges

Thomas Edison famously remarked that 'genius is one percent inspiration and ninety-nine percent perspiration'. There have been many creative thinkers since who have said similar things, indicating that it is their resilience and stubborn refusal to accept defeat that makes creative people successful in the end. If at first you don't succeed, try, try again, as the old adage goes.

Such resilience, so necessary for creativity to survive and thrive, needs to be encouraged through school, and the only way to do this is to present the children with situations in which they need to show resilience. So the pupils need to be presented with challenges in which they can use their creativity to see a way out of a problem and then, crucially, use their resilience to keep going even when it seems like they are failing to make progress.

'Necessity is the mother of invention' is a proverb often ascribed to Plato. Difficult situations can indeed inspire some innovative thinking and the children need to be given the opportunity to think their way out of a problem. The question, of course, is what kinds of problem can we present to the children that will inspire some ingenious creativity whilst, at the same time, keeping their self-confidence and optimism intact.

The truth is, there is opportunity to present pupils with head-scratching problems every day – in the way we present the curriculum to them, every lesson.

By virtue of being human, all children have a propensity for meaning-making – finding out what something means, and whether it contains a threat or a benefit to them. We can present information to them in ways which encourage this meaning-making.

Such challenges might include:

- here is the answer, what is the question?

- this is the correct answer, but can you reach it via a different method?

- can you reword a statement or sentence so that it still conveys the same meaning?

- can you reword a statement or sentence so that it conveys the opposite meaning?

- here is the destination, how did I get there?

- can you think of some new acronyms for well-known, established ones (e.g. NASA, DfE, AWOL, SOS, DOB, AKA, UFO, TBC).

- if you could be Headteacher of our school for a day, what changes to the school would you introduce?

- if you could be Prime Minister for a day, what changes to the country would you introduce?

- if the school won a grant of £100,000 and you were in charge, how would you spend it?

- if you won £1,000,000 how would you spend it?

- plan a presentation for a younger class on why examinations matter

- plan a presentation for a younger class on why examinations don't matter

- write down ten important character traits of a good teacher

- put together a guide to surviving and thriving through school

- write down a sentence to explain the word 'creativity'

- how many different words can you make using the letters on the top row of a keyboard?

- how many different ways can you make the number 5 in thirty seconds?

Like all elements of the invisible curriculum, creativity is best encouraged by placing before the children choices and challenges in which they have the opportunity to exercise some independent thinking and for which there is no immediately obvious right or wrong answer. There is nothing so motivational than being able to decide for oneself how or when to approach a particular problem – drawing on one's own experience and knowledge in order to take control and produce something you can feel proud of. The above challenges require some thinking and they are open to interpretation. The key skill is to be able to justify your answer.

7

The element of doubt

In *Craft* (2000), Professor Phillip Gammage is quoted for suggesting that education, rather than focusing on 'answering the question', should instead be focusing on the importance of 'questioning the answer'.

There is a shift in emphasis here from the more traditional model of teacher as all-knowing expert and child as passive recipient, to one of Socratic dialogue and shared discovery. Of course, there will be many times when knowledge is indubitable and universal truths need to be learned by the pupil, but from a creativity standpoint, divergent thinking is of great benefit and allows the child to come to knowledge themselves, make their own connections and perhaps even form new conclusions. We cannot assume that everything we tell the children is not open to scrutiny and challenge, just as we cannot assume that everything we learned in school was correct – as we get older we find that some of it manifestly was not!

The element of doubt is a very useful tool when encouraging creative thinking in school because it keeps curiosity alive, unlike certainty which kills it dead.

Curiosity and possibility thinking are of great value to the teaching of creativity. We must be encouraging the children to question answers and challenge them. We want them to suggest new ways of doing things, new ways of thinking and solving problems. The element of doubt is an essential tool for this precisely because it leaves open the possibility of doing things differently.

Let me give you an example, with the assistance of Ian Gilbert's tremendous book, *The Little Book of Thunks* (2007). According to Gilbert, a *Thunk* is 'a beguilingly simple-looking question about every day things that stops you in your tracks and helps you start looking at the world in a whole new light.' The book contains 260 of these questions, one of which is:

> 226. If I gave you a lump of mud to play with would it be a toy? If yes, would it be a toy when you stopped playing with it? Was it a toy before you started playing with it? (Gilbert, 2007: 82)

You could answer this question with a straight, 'No, it's not a toy and it never was because it was never built as a toy.'

Job done. But there is still a tantalising element of doubt here. The Oxford English Dictionary defines a toy as 'an object for a child to play with.' If a child is playing with the lump of mud, then surely it is a toy, albeit an improvised one. But if you take that as a rule, then anything can be a toy if a child plays with it, which clearly is nonsense. A child can play with a dog and that doesn't make it a toy. Or a child can play with my Aunty Beryl and that doesn't make her toy. Or a child can play with the petals on a flower and that doesn't make it a toy – it's a plant.

In my experience, children will often react to questions like these with an immediate 'yes' or 'no'. But when we encourage them to think a little more, the element of doubt creeps in and it is this which allows them to grapple with it, perceive new possibilities and drawbacks, and create scenarios to test the validity of their original view.

Here is another Thunk which I have often used with children:

> 68. Is the gap between the notes, music? (Gilbert, 2007: 43)

Many children will immediately say 'No, of course it's not.' But if you point out that without the gaps (or rests) the music would sound very different, then some children will see that the rests must be part of the music. If that is the case then, is a minute's silence a form of music? Or if you ended a song with four bars of silence, when did the song actually finish – when you stopped playing? When did the silence finish – when the audience applauded? And did the silence resume after that?

And finally, here is a third Thunk which has sparked many debates with my classes over the years:

54. If I read a comic in a shop without paying for it is that stealing? (Gilbert, 2007: 40)

If you have not removed the comic from the shop at all, then it is hard to see how you have committed a theft. It was still in the shop when you left, after all. But you have taken something, surely? If the purpose of a comic is to provide pictures to look at and words to read, and you have seen those pictures and read those words, without paying any money for any of them, then you have stolen something, haven't you?

I am a fan of philosophical questions such as these because they encourage children to grapple with them, free of the fear of 'getting it wrong'. The element of doubt gives permission to the children to think for themselves and to come up with their own conclusions, which may be different to their teachers' or their peers' views. That is very good news for creativity.

Martin Cohen's *101 Philosophy Problems* provides similar conundrums that can stimulate some creative thinking in class. One such problem is a favourite of mine and it has prompted some long debates with children:

> At last! Something that is definite. The statement on the other side of this piece of paper is *true*.
>
> (On the reverse side, it reads):
> The claim on the other side of this piece of paper is *false*.
> (Cohen, 1999: 13-14)

Good luck with that one. I have spent many lessons watching children grapple over whether both statements can co-exist. In one discussion the children all decided that, in theory, the piece of paper should not exist at all and should really have spontaneously combusted.

When incorporating the element of doubt into creative discussions, I have often found the following scenarios very productive, which I may have made up myself or read in a book somewhere, I really can't remember now.

Scenario 1

The stationery cupboard in the corner of the classroom is not actually a cupboard at all; it is a time machine. I have been grappling with this business of time travel and have managed to build my own, rather basic, time machine. I set the dial to a week's time – the same lesson the following week. I invite the children to join me, saying who's going to come with me into the future? The technology is still pretty clunky – I am not a genius scientist, after all – but it does work. It will take approximately seven days to reach the destination.

When one of the bright sparks tells me 'That's not a time machine, Sir, that's cupboard. If we went in there and waited for seven days, we'd not be stepping out into the future, we'd be stepping out into the present,' I say the following:

'If I improved the technology and it took us only three minutes to travel to this time next week, would that be a proper time machine?'

Most children chorus their approval.

'Okay,' I say,' 'Let's imagine we take that three-minute journey together. We will still be stepping out into our present, because we will have experienced the three minutes it took to get there – so it's not our future, it's our present, three minutes later. Everyone else we see around us will be experiencing life in their present too – so in what way is that a trip to the future? How is that a better time machine?'

Scenario 2

The stationery cupboard in the corner of the classroom is not actually a cupboard at all; it is an operating theatre. I have been grappling with this business of brain surgery and have finally managed to identify and isolate the 'sad gene' which enables us to feel sad. By removing it I can render your default setting 'always happy'. The operation is perfectly painless, using laser surgery, and takes just twenty minutes. So who would like to have the operation?

The discussions that follow are always enlightening. I have only ever found one child who was ready to have the operation, everyone else refuses. The most common reason given is that if they can no longer feel sadness, they cannot feel empathy and would therefore lose their friends eventually. When I have replied with, 'Yes, and you'll be happy about that,' they have never seemed convinced. Other children have said that an inability to feel sadness might mask our sense of pain and so therefore we might injure ourselves because we don't mind the pain. This could lead to serious injury. Again, I have said, 'Yes, and you'll be happy about that, but they have still not been convinced. It's that old animal, survival brain again!

Here are some useful question starters to help you imply an element of doubt and present information to the children in ways which still leave room for them to question and challenge and come up with new, creative thoughts and hypotheses:

- Imagine if...

- Let's hypothesise that...

- What would have happened if...

- Do you think that...

- Why should...

- Why do you think...

- Some people believe that...

- Do you agree with...

- If we conducted an experiment into...

- What do you think will happen if...

- If the world was flat...

And here are some questions that will encourage the children to look at things differently and consider every day events and objects from a more creative viewpoint:

- Does a bird know it's a bird? Does it matter whether it knows or not?

- Some movies are described as 3D. What would a film need to offer for it to be called a genuine 4D movie?

- Is there such a thing as free will? If you choose sponge and custard instead of yoghurt at lunch today were you always destined to choose that? Was it pre-ordained? If you decide to 'beat destiny' and suddenly switch to yoghurt right at the last minute, weren't you always destined to make that last-minute switch?

- If you prefer one piece of music over another, where do you feel that? Where is that preference felt inside your body?

- Is my green the same as your green? Or is it bluer than yours?

- What colour is Tuesday?

- If an alien asked you to describe what it means to be human, what would you say?

- Is there such a thing as the future, really? What about the past?

- We are living through an age that has seen more advances in science and technology than ever before in our history. So why are people starving?

- We are living in age when there are more billionaires on the planet than ever before, so why are people living in poverty?

- If there weren't such a thing as God or multiple gods, what would people believe in?

- If everyone on the planet believed in one God would you still need faith?

- Is happiness real? Is sadness real? Can you have one without the other? Which is there more of in the world, happiness or sadness?

- How can a computer ever be cleverer than the people who made it?

- How should progress be measured in school? In numbers, letters, percentages, achievements, friendships or smiles? Or something else altogether? What does *progress* actually mean?

- What does it mean to have a 'successful education'? Can you describe one?

Questions of this nature suggest that there is more than one 'correct' answer and they also invite the children to look again at common acceptances in their lives and find that they are not as definite or beyond criticism as they first thought. They may find new ways of looking at things, and ultimately new answers.

Possessing an ability and a willingness to look at things afresh, to question the purpose and value of things we often take for granted, is an important part of being creative. Unless we introduce that element of doubt – through questions such as those above – some children may never question how and why we live our lives the way we do. And that's how progress is halted.

8 Observation

Observation is a key element to the creative process and yet it can so easily affect the result. Consider the teacher moving around the room, peering over the shoulders of the children as they draw their picture or write their poem. We have huge impact on the children's productivity, their confidence in their own ability and their willingness to plunge in and have a go.

There is little we can do about that, save leaving the room every time we ask the children to create something. We cannot be absent from the creative process, but we can make our presence a positive, motivational force by providing positive feedback and words of encouragement as much as possible. This is our role.

I have stated before in this book how we can assess the children's developing skills in creativity – their ability to write, draw, paint, design, problem-solve and think creatively. We can do this without passing judgement on their imagination. Technical skills can be modelled and then assessed in the children through the work they produce.

What is especially interesting to consider is how we observe the children's creativity developing – their ability to perceive, connect, synthesise and present the novel thoughts and ideas they have in their minds – without affecting the outcome.

As I mentioned in Chapter 4, it seems sensible to focus on creative behaviour rather than exclusively on the creative product produced, and to emphasise the child's ownership of their work. In the verbal or written feedback we should use phrases which drive this point home – and I have referenced those in Chapter 4

– *eg* using phrases like 'I admire your decision to...', 'I like your choice of...' and 'I am impressed by your use of...'. The word 'your' is key if we are to encourage the children to invest in the creative process and realise that they can express themselves how they want to and be judged not on whether they are right or wrong, but on how much they have tried.

When giving any feedback it is always important to have already ascertained the success criteria – the aims for the creative project. When it comes to creativity in school, this must be in part down to the child: the brief they set themselves from the outset and the image they had in their mind at the point when the creative impulse struck. We can use this to judge whether a creative activity has proved successful or not. Encouraging the children to critique their own work – sensibly and positively – is a crucial part of any creative education.

If we are lucky, we all have creative, epiphanic moments from time to time. What makes us successful is how we listen to that voice inside of us when creative inspiration strikes and how disciplined we are from that point on. Are we able to follow through on an idea, even beyond the moment when the initial euphoria fades, which it always does. Are we able to stick with it and see it through to the end? These behaviours, such as resilience, commitment, determination, self-belief, hard work, can and should be commented upon within the teacher observation.

Notice I am saying *observation* here, rather than *assessment*. It would be difficult to attach a numbered or lettered assessment grade to these creative traits and attitudes, wouldn't it, and it may drag us back to a fixed mindset once again. We would need to alter that grade every time the children return to the project, since we all greet creative work in fits and starts, enjoying moments when it flows easily and enduring those others when we feel uninspired. How do you grade that?

I believe you ask the children to consider how they have learned from the difficult moments, how have they grown from them. If creativity was all plain sailing from the moment of the initial perception to the final presentation then it would be difficult to grow from the experience and find strength for future projects, surely.

The DfE's Teachers' Standards require us to 'give pupils regular feedback, both orally and through accurate marking, and encourage pupils to respond to the feedback.' This final part of the requirement is important for us here. We need to encourage the children to offer their own responses, both to the work they have done personally and to the work of others. Again, it is sensible to focus on creative behaviour rather than creative skills alone.

I introduced the term 'creactivity' earlier in the book and it is worth returning to it here in our discussion on observation. Creactivity needs that creative spark, that energising moment of creative inspiration, and what is very interesting from an assessment point of view is to observe what happens next and not allow our own assessment procedures to intrude (I'm thinking again of the waiter in the restaurant, asking us how our food is, just when we would like to be left alone to enjoy it).

Had I stopped Henry during his frenzy of writing books on Nelson and HMS Victory to ask him what he was doing, if he was he feeling confident, could he talk me through his plans and give an assessment of whether he thought he would achieve them or not, then I'm sure his self-motivation to create, create, create would have quickly diminished. We would have lost the moment. Perhaps the last thing he would have wanted to do at that time was provide a running commentary on the creative process or, even worse, receive a running commentary from me on his progress. Perish the thought!

But catching the children being creative and storing up questions to ask them once the creative process is over is certainly worth doing.

Such questions may include:

- Has what you have made matched up to your expectations?
- Is this what you had in your mind when you started on the creative journey?
- How might you do things differently next time?
- Are you pleased with what you have created? If not, why not?
- What have you learned during the creative process:

    a) about the skills involved?

    b) about yourself?

- Would you have liked to have had more time? How would you have used it?
- How would you rate your creative skills in this field?
- How would you rate your creative behaviour on this project?

- What sort of attitudes and traits do you think you need to be creative? Or is it just down to skill?

- Has this creative product expressed what you wanted to say to the world?

- What mistakes did you make along the way and how have you learned form them?

- Can you describe what a creative person is like? What makes them especially creative do you think?

Once the children are in a position to consider how they have performed, and once we, as teacher, are ready to do so too, it is worth breaking the process into its four stages – perceiving, connecting, synthesising and presenting – so that we can assess the extent to which the child has succeeded in each stage, and the extent to which they feel they have succeeded.

Some suggestions for this follow. I have used a sliding scale of 1 to 10 for these self-assessment questions, as I feel when it comes to self-assessment, grades and numbers do have a value. I am less keen to award an assessment grade as a teacher, because so much of the creative process is subjective – you will remember I quoted Freud in Chapter 2: creativity originates in a 'conflict within the unconscious mind'. As I said earlier, not only is an internal moment of creative inspiration difficult for observers to understand and report on, such an epiphany may even be difficult for the creator himself to express in words. As Ken Robinson puts it, typically eloquently:

Trying to put some experiences into words is like stringing clothes out on a washing line when in practice they are worn one inside the other.' (2001: 122).

Enabling children to retrace their steps and articulate to others 'what happened' in the creative process is an important part of observing and assessing creativity. This way they can learn from mistakes, gain confidence from triumphs and know how to recognise creative inspiration when it comes again. Allowing the children to 'grade' their work and behaviour is somehow more palatable than having a teacher place a grade on it, because there is a certain authority and judgement inherent in the formal, teacher assessment which communicates a fixed mindset, whether we like it or not.

A Self Assessment for a Creative Project

Now that you have completed this creative project, on a scale of 1 to 10, how would you rate the following skills and attitudes?

Circle the number you think most accurately reflects your ability at the moment (Remember: you can always get better next time!)

Stage 1: Perceiving

How would you rate your sensory perception on this project?

(Using your senses to prepare for this project, noticing what is around you and engaging with what you have to work with)

| 1 | 2 | 3 | 4 | 5 | 6 | 7 | 8 | 9 | 10 |

Stage 2: Connecting

How would you rate your ability to make new connections on this project?

(Using your imagination to make new links and new patterns based on the resources you have around you)

| 1 | 2 | 3 | 4 | 5 | 6 | 7 | 8 | 9 | 10 |

Stage 3: Synthesising

How would you rate your technical skills on this project?

(Using your skills and knowledge to build something original)

| 1 | 2 | 3 | 4 | 5 | 6 | 7 | 8 | 9 | 10 |

Stage 4: Presenting

How would you rate your ability to present your project to others?

(Explaining the process you followed, what you intended and how you achieved it)

| 1 | 2 | 3 | 4 | 5 | 6 | 7 | 8 | 9 | 10 |

Conclusion

Like all aspects of the invisible curriculum, creativity needs to be planned. Perhaps it requires carefully structured planning more than any other part of the children's 'invisible ink' because it is so often associated with a lack of structure. In the regular visits I make to schools to consult on creativity in the curriculum, I often drive home the point that creativity can and should be planned; it need not rely solely on those spontaneous moments of creative inspiration that come drifting through the window from time to time.

But how? How do we plan for the children to 'be creative' on demand? I have spent many years grappling with this one and, though the creative person in me may feel hard done by at the prospect of concluding this book with a reference to the work of another, I cannot find a better model for planning creativity in school than that which is found within Michael Gelb's excellent book, *How to think like da Vinci* (1998).

Gelb identifies seven 'da Vincian principles'. Though I am sure these were never intended to be taken as a guide for how to plan for creativity in school – the book is by no means aimed at educators alone – such principles could reinvigorate our planning systems and enrich our teaching and learning most effectively.

When I deliver CPD courses on creativity I usually ask colleagues to close their eyes and imagine the great master whispering these words to them, down through the centuries. I recite each one in probably the worst Italian accent you have ever heard, but I think they get the point. I am proud to be one sixteenth

Italian, my distant ancestors originate from Lake Como, which in my book is as good as saying I have direct lineage to the master himself.

Dear reader, if you close your eyes you won't be able to read these so I suggest you don't. And I cannot whisper them to you, which may come as a relief to many. But I do suggest that you use your imagination to picture Leonardo whispering these into your ear, begging you to pass them on to your students, so that generations more will enjoy the thrill of what it means to live a creative life. Hear his raspy voice. Imagine him breathing each word to you, through the generations. He is persuading you to stay curious, keep an open mind, don't give up asking and challenging and searching. Don't settle for the usual answers, search beyond them, seek out new ones. Enjoy the spontaneous.

As you read these principles, decide how you will incorporate each one into your planning tomorrow, next week, next term.

Curiosità – An insatiably curious approach to life and an unrelenting quest for continuous learning.

Dimostrazione – A commitment to test knowledge through experience, persistence, and a willingness to learn from mistakes.

Sensazione – The continual refinement of the senses, especially sight, as the means to enliven experience.

Sfumato (literally 'Going up in smoke') – A willingness to embrace ambiguity, paradox, and uncertainty.

Arte/Scienza – The development of the balance between science and art, logic and imagination. 'Whole brain' thinking.

Corporalita – The cultivation of grace, ambidexterity, fitness and poise.

Connessione – A recognition of an appreciation for the interconnectedness of all things and phenomena. Systems thinking. (Gelb, 1998: 9)

As Gelb points out, the most distinctive trait of highly creative people is *Sfumato*, the ability to embrace uncertainty and the unknown. Indeed, Gelb suggests that 'Leonardo probably had more of that trait than anyone who has ever lived.'

Schools are, by nature, places of certainty – with rigid timetables, planned lessons and a compartmentalised curriculum. Life outside school is less certain, far less predictable. But I shall not leap on the usual bandwagon and suggest that life is fraught with dangers and difficulties and so therefore school should be harder and less comfortable for the children, to build up their character and get them used to the school-for-hard-knocks that awaits them beyond the gate. School is already a hard experience to endure, we don't need to make it any harder.

But we can fill it with the joy of surprises and uncertainties from time to time. And we can use the time together to sharpen up our senses and remind one another what it means to be a human being, for whom senses are more vital, ultimately, than computational capacity and the ability to apply logic.

The children who begin school this year will still be working well beyond 2075 and a great many of them will see the turn of the next century. The knowledge and concepts they learn in school will help to shape their view of the world, but it is their creativity that will help them to change the world. It is the extent to which they embrace creative thinking and creative doing that will determine how much they contribute to this century and how much they get out of it. No one knows what the world of work or leisure will look like in fifty or sixty years' time, but one thing is certain, there will be large-scale changes to embrace and problems to be solved. Today's pupils will not be adequately equipped for them simply by learning the knowledge that we hand to them, which in turn was handed to us by the teachers who taught us, and which came from the teachers who taught them, and the teachers who taught them.

To repeat the mantra once again, it is not a question of *either* academic teaching *or* creative play, it is *and*. It must be.

But if Leonardo were to visit one of our classrooms today I feel sure he would be pleasantly surprised. There is plenty of creativity going on – lots of creactivity.

The trick is to notice it more readily, celebrate it, and recognise the four steps involved in the creative process so that we can make a conscious effort to be better at each one. Future generations will need their creativity far more than we realise, so it is time to spell out what that elusive, capricious word actually means.

And it's time to buy your children a button box.

References

Almond, D. (1998) *Skellig*. London: Hodder Children's Books.

Buck, P. S. quoted in Inglesias, K. (2001) *The 101 Habits of Highly Successful Screenwriters*. USA: Adams Media.

Claxton, P. (2008) *What's the Point of School?* Oxford: Oneworld Publications.

Cohen, M. (1999) *101 Philosophy Problems*. London: Routledge.

Cowley, S. (2005) *Letting the Buggers be Creative*. London: Continuum.

Craft, A. (2005) *Creativity in Schools – Tensions and Dilemmas*. London: Routledge.

Fisher, R. (2004) *Unlocking Creativity*. London: David Fulton .

Joubert, M. M. (2001) 'The Art of Creative Teaching'. In Craft, A. (2001) (Ed) *Creativity in Education*. London: Continuum.

Gamez, G. (2006) *How to Catch Lightning in a Bottle*. Mumbai: Jaico Publishing House.

Gammage, P. (2000) cited in Craft, A. (2000) *Creativity across the primary curriculum*. London: Routledge.

Gelb, M. (1998) *How to think like Leonardo da Vinci*. London: Thorsons, Harper Collins.

Gilbert, I. (2007) *The Little Book of Thunks*. Camarthen, Wales: Crown House Publishing Ltd.

Golden, B. (2007) *Unlock Your Creative Genius*. New York: Prometheus Books.

Jobs, S. (1996) featured in Wired Magazine, Boone, IA, USA.

Klass, D. (2001) *You Don't Know Me*. London: Viking, Penguin Group.

Kneller, G. F. (1965) *The Art and Science of Creativity*. New York: Holt, Rinehart and Winston.

Mean, L. A. (2006) *On Creativity: Awakening the Creative Mind*. Malaysia: Pelanduk Publications.

Novak, J. (1998) *Learning, Creating and Using Knowledge*. New Jersey: Lawrence Eribaum Associates.

Robinson, K. (2000) featured in 'All our futures'. National Advisory Committee on Creative and Cultural Education.

Robinson, K. (2001) *Out of Our Minds: Learning to be Creative*. Chichester: Capstone Publishing Ltd.

Stein, M. I. (1984) *Anecdotes, Poems and Illustrations for the Creative Process: Making the Point*. Bearly Ltd: USA.

Also Available

INK
THE INVISIBLE
INK SERIES

TEACHING FOR CHARACTER

SUPER-CHARGED LEARNING
THROUGH THE
'INVISIBLE CURRICULUM'

ANDREW HAMMOND

Order online from
www.johncattbookshop.com
£10

Forthcoming titles in the Invisible Ink series

Teaching for Motivation

Teaching for Curiosity

Teaching for Thinking Skills

Teaching for Communication

Teaching for Interdependence